THE SOUND OF ONE TEAM SUCKING

THE SOUND OF ONE TEAM SUCKING

Mindful Meditations for Recovering Leafs Fans

Christopher Gudgeon

with Tavish Gudgeon, Joey Mauro, and Yusuf Saadi

DUNDURN
TORONTO

Copyright © Christopher Gudgeon, 2017

All rights reserved. No part of this publication may be reproduced, stored in a retrieval system, or transmitted in any form or by any means, electronic, mechanical, photocopying, recording, or otherwise (except for brief passages for purposes of review) without the prior permission of Dundurn Press. Permission to photocopy should be requested from Access Copyright.

This book is not affiliated with Maple Leaf Sports and Entertainment, the Toronto Maple Leafs, or the National Hockey League. Any errors or omissions are the responsibility of the authors.

Cover image credit: istockphoto.com/ filo
Printer: Webcom

Library and Archives Canada Cataloguing in Publication

Gudgeon, Chris, 1959-, author
    The sound of one team sucking : mindful meditations for recovering Leafs fans / Christopher Gudgeon with Tavish Gudgeon, Joey Mauro, and Yusuf Saadi.

Issued in print and electronic formats.
ISBN 978-1-4597-3835-5 (softcover).--ISBN 978-1-4597-3836-2 (PDF).--ISBN 978-1-4597-3837-9 (EPUB)

1. Toronto Maple Leafs (Hockey team)--Humor. I. Gudgeon, Tavish, author II. Mauro, Joey, 1996-, author III. Saadi, Yusuf, author IV. Title.

GV848.T6G83 2017   796.962'6409713541   C2016-907750-0
                                                                                                                                        C2016-907751-9

1 2 3 4 5   21   20 19 18 17

We acknowledge the support of the **Canada Council for the Arts** and the **Ontario Arts Council** for our publishing program. We also acknowledge the financial support of the **Government of Ontario**, through the **Ontario Book Publishing Tax Credit** and the **Ontario Media Development Corporation**, and the **Government of Canada**.

Care has been taken to trace the ownership of copyright material used in this book. The author and the publisher welcome any information enabling them to rectify any references or credits in subsequent editions.
— *J. Kirk Howard, President*

The publisher is not responsible for websites or their content unless they are owned by the publisher.

VISIT US AT

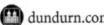 dundurn.com | @dundurnpress | dundurnpress | dundurnpress

Dundurn
3 Church Street, Suite 500
Toronto, Ontario, Canada
M5E 1M2

This book is dedicated to Jim Ralph.

As a player, his talent was only exceeded by his goals against average; as a broadcaster, his relentless dedication to the sport and his uncanny ability to get repeatedly fired as the Leafs colour commentator is an inspiration to recovering Leafs fans everywhere.

Also dedicated to Riley Gudgeon, proving that, while money can't buy happiness, it can buy a shout out in this book.

*God, grant me the serenity to accept
the things I cannot change,
courage to change the things I can,
and wisdom to know the difference.
And also: please, God ... don't let Auston Matthews be a bust.*

— from "The Serenity Prayer" (sort of) by Karl Niebuhr,
ethicist, theologian, and, quite possibly, recovering Leafs fan

INTRODUCTION

What is the sound of one team sucking?

> *Trying to understand is like straining through muddy water. Have the patience to wait! Be still and allow the mud to settle.*
>
> — Lao Tzu, Chinese philosopher and spiritual father to the Shanaplan

We've all heard it. The sound of one team sucking. Our team: the Toronto Maple Leafs.

It starts as an almost imperceptible hum a month or so after the home opener, once the excitement of a new season wears off.

It builds in intensity with each defeat until, sometime after the All-Star break, the sound explodes — an internalized shriek like the noise a star might make if you ripped its heart out.

It's a ritual for us.

We start the season with cautious optimism and, as training camp approaches, we promise ourselves that, this time around, we won't get carried away. Then the season starts and the Leafs win a few games, maybe even put together an impressive winning streak. It's still early, we tell ourselves: let's not get too excited.

But we slowly get swept up and, even as the losses pile up and the playoff prospects grow dimmer and dimmer, we are confident that this time the team will turn it around. And then things come unhinged: our scorers stop scoring, our goalies turn into human Swiss cheese, the power play looks more like a power failure.

When the inevitable happens and the Leafs are mathematically eliminated, once again, we hit rock bottom. Another season, which began with such promise, has ended in heartbreak.

The Leafs are not going to let us down again, we tell ourselves.

We endured Harold Ballard …

We put up with countless bad trades and ill-advised free agent signings.

We have survived the longest-standing Stanley Cup drought, almost half a century of futility.

The time has come to stop caring; stop wearing our Maple Leafs underwear to work; stop checking the blogs for reports on pimple-faced prospects playing for Yunost Minsk or the Notre Dame Hounds; stop worrying about which players are overpaid, who should be traded, and why.

And we're fine … for a while. But then it happens, usually around draft day: we open our minds and hearts to the possibility that is the Toronto Maple Leafs. And the cycle begins again.

Let's face it, we have a problem. The fact is, being a Leafs fan is a kind of addiction: irrational, compulsive, dependent. We can't just stop cold turkey. We need help. And that's where *The Sound of One Team Sucking* comes in. Think of it as your own portable support group, designed to stand by you through another disappointing season (plus draft day!), help you maintain your focus and perspective, and guide your recovery as — in the face of the Leafs' certain futility — you strive to live a more emotionally and spiritually balanced life.

It's going to be a long season, but with this book, you're going to make it through ...

GAME 1

A journey of a single step starts with a thousand excuses.

— "Sugar" Roy Carboyle, self-help guru and world's foremost demotivational psychologist

12 Steps for Recovering Leafs Fans

1. Admit to ourselves that we have an irrational and uncontrollable obsession with the Toronto Maple Leafs.
2. Admit to our friends and loved ones that we have a serious Leafs jones going on.
3. Understand that only a power greater than ourselves — some combination of Brendan Shanahan and Auston Matthews — can restore us to sanity.
4. Turn our lives and team over to the care of "Shanahews" as we understand him.
5. Make a searching and fearless moral inventory of ourselves, or at least a short list of the slightly irritating Leafs-related things we do that bug our friends.
6. Continue to take personal inventories and when we are

wrong (like, oh I don't know, trading two first-rounders and a second-rounder for Phil Kessel), promptly admit it (come on, Burkie).
7. Cancel our subscription to Leafs TV.
8. Humbly ask Shanahews to remove our shortcomings, or at least stick to the Shanaplan.
9. Make a list of all persons we have harmed and become willing to make amends with them all ... unless they are Canucks fans.
10. Make direct amends with these people wherever possible, except if doing so would injure them (or if they are Canucks fans, in which case they can just go screw themselves).
11. Improve through mindful meditation our conscious contact with Shanahews, and pray that He has the wisdom and power to stick to the goddamned plan this time.
12. Having had a spiritual awakening as a result of following these steps, carry this message to other recovering Leafs fans because, you know, misery loves company.

GAME DAY AFFIRMATION

Today I will commit myself to my recovery, to the 12 Steps, and to the Shanaplan as I understand it.

GAME 2

> *Q: What do the Toronto Maple Leafs and the* Titanic *have in common?*
>
> *A: They both look good until they hit the ice!*

You've done it. You've admitted you have a problem. A big blue-and-white monkey off your back.

You almost had it beat at the end of last season. Summer came (early, of course, for us Leafs fans), and the sunshine and light almost made you forget about those long, dark winters of the soul.

But here you are again. Glued to your TV, smartphone, or computer, waiting for the puck to drop on another Leafs season.

This time, you tell yourself, it's going to be different. After all, they made some pretty good trades in the off-season, signed a couple good free agents. And the new president/GM/coach/captain is promising more commitment/truculence/effort/intensity. What could go wrong? We've got this.

Things have to change, right? I mean, the new leadership has a clear strategic vision — like the Shanaplan — in place, right? And the Leafs have lost for long enough; they're bound to have a championship season, right? This is our year.

Not necessarily. Consider the case of baseball's Chicago Cubs. After winning their second consecutive World Series in 1908, they didn't win another championship for eighty-eight years. It was the worst dry spell of any team in the big four professional sports leagues — Major League Baseball, the National Football League, the National Basketball Association, and the National Hockey League — and kind of puts the Leafs' paltry failures into perspective.

As recovering Leafs fans, we are swept up in the ritual, the annual sacrament of anticipation and disappointment. It's like a drug for us, providing a certain certainty in an uncertain universe.

We must learn to move past the tyranny of expectation. It's a kind of desire, and, as the Buddhists tell us, desire is the root of all suffering. The key is to understand that, while hope has value (because it makes us focus on the process), expectation is an illusion: it forces us to focus on outcomes, which we cannot control, and blinds us to what is happening in the moment.

GAME DAY AFFIRMATION

Today I will allow myself to be optimistic about the upcoming season, while recognizing that this optimism is ridiculously misguided.

GAME 3

> *The past is your lesson, the present your gift, the future your motivation.*
>
> — Anonymous, internet hacker and quote machine

Being a Leafs fan has never been easy. In fact, things were tough even before the Leafs were the Leafs. Take the team's very first franchise owner, Eddie Livingstone, for example. He was a blustery renegade, whose off-ice antics would have given Harold Ballard a run for his embezzled money.

Livingstone entered the picture in 1914. After a successful stint in amateur sports — his Toronto Rugby and Amateur Association team won the Ontario Hockey Association senior championships two years in a row — he bought the Toronto Ontarios of the National Hockey Association (NHA), precursor to the NHL. Livingstone got rid of the Ontarios' gaudy orange sweater, dressed them in emerald green, and the Toronto Shamrocks were born.

Livingstone had a number of legendary battles with players, co-owners, and the press. One of his most famous feuds involved the legendary Cy Denneny, the leading scorer on Livingstone's rechristened Toronto Blueshirts team. After getting a civil service job in Ottawa, Denneny demanded a trade to the Senators.

Livingstone first refused, then — faced with Denneny's threat to sit out the season — capitulated in Ballardian fashion, asking for either Frank Nighbor, the Senators' star player, or the unheard-of sum of $1,800 in return. Livingstone finally settled on a lesser player and $750 for Denneny, but the damage was done. Livingstone lost his best player, and the Senators gained a star who would help them win four Stanley Cups over the next dozen years.

Livingstone followed this disaster by publicly bad-mouthing amateur star Lionel Conacher, one of the most famous athletes in the country, because the player refused to sign a pro contract with Toronto.

After Livingstone questioned his character, Canada's future Top Athlete of the Half Century successfully sued … and then went on to enjoy a great NHL career, without ever playing a game for his hometown Toronto team.

GAME DAY AFFIRMATION

Today I will remind myself that for every Harold Ballard, there is an Eddie Livingstone waiting to take his place.

GAME 4

> *Every adversity, every failure, every heartache carries with it the seed of an equal or greater benefit.*
>
> — Napoleon Hill, inspirational author and notorious aphorism thief

Despite his contrary nature — or perhaps *because* of it — Eddie Livingstone turned out to be one of the pivotal figures in NHL history.

The year was 1915 and Livingstone was now the proud owner of two Toronto-based NHA franchises: the Shamrocks and the Blueshirts. He'd purchased the latter the previous year, thinking that if he owned both teams, he could avoid bidding wars and pay his players less.

The league board wasn't happy with the arrangement. One Livingstone team was enough; two teams gave him two votes at the board meetings, and that was two votes too many.

So the league ordered Livingstone to get rid of one of the teams. To no one's surprise, he refused, so they eventually took over the Shamrocks and mothballed the team, dispersing the players across the league.

The following season, the NHA replaced the Shamrocks with a team made up of members of the 228th Battalion, stationed near Toronto and boasting a number of Livingstone's former players. Even as the team took to the ice for its first game — the players dressed in their army-issued khakis — Livingstone was protesting the result.

Halfway through the season, the 228th Battalion was sent overseas to fight in the First World War. Left with just five teams, the league held a meeting without Livingstone. Tired of the Toronto owner's antics (and wanting an even number of teams for scheduling reasons) the NHA directors voted to suspend the Blueshirts, triggering a spate of lawsuits and countersuits.

In February 1917, the owners had another meeting, once again neglecting to add Livingstone to the guest list. This time, they came up with a simple but elegant solution to their Blueshirts problem: shut the entire league down, which they did. A few weeks later, the same group announced the formation of the new National Hockey League: same owners, same teams, same rules as the old NHA, but 100 percent Livingstone-free.

GAME DAY AFFIRMATION

Today I will contemplate the simple wisdom of the NHA and remind myself that adversity, like necessity, can be the mother of invention (or in this case, re-invention).

GAME 5

> *Never confuse movement with action.*
>
> — Ernest Hemingway, author and gifted self-parodist

As we travel the road to recovery, we often take one step forward and two steps back. It's the way progress works in both hockey and in life.

Consider the story of the creation of the Toronto St. Patricks, the direct precursor to the Maple Leafs.

The St. Pats started out as the Toronto Arenas, the city's non–Eddie Livingstone franchise. The team was part of the company that owned the Arena Gardens, the main rink in Toronto at the time. The company was granted a temporary franchise in 1917, and leased its players from the Toronto Blueshirts, then under suspension because the team owner, Livingstone, was — *surprise!* — involved in another acrimonious legal battle with the NHL at the time.

The Arenas turned out to be a darned good team, winning the Stanley Cup in only their second season — and the owners enjoyed the taste of victory so much that they decided to renege on their deal with Livingstone and keep all the players they'd borrowed from the Blueshirts.

Big mistake. Livingstone, of course, sued the Arena Company, and was awarded a $20,000 settlement — an enormous sum at the time. Rather than paying Livingstone, the team owners declared bankruptcy, and that franchise story could have ended there.

But fate stepped in, in the form of Arenas GM Charlie Querrie, who took over the franchise, changed its name to the Tecumsehs — in honour of a famous Shawnee warrior — and then turned around and the very next day sold the whole team to a local amateur club called the St. Patricks.

It was one small step that moved Toronto closer to the mecca of Leafs Nation. Now all that was needed was a couple steps back.

GAME DAY AFFIRMATION

Today I will remind myself that neither Rome nor the Maple Leafs were built in a day, and that progress is a process, not a destination.

GAME 6

I've got nothing to say, and I'm only going to say it once!

— Floyd Smith, former Leafs coach and
one-man verbal wrecking crew

As recovering Leafs fans, we've already taken the critical first steps to admitting we have a problem. While there might not be a Leafs Anonymous to help us (note to self: copyright Leafs Anonymous), there are things we can do to help our recovery. As a starting point, it's helpful to understand the exact nature of our problem.

How bad is your Leafs dependency? Take this simple test to find out:

1. As the season approached, did you find yourself growing more and more preoccupied with the Leafs at the expense of other aspects of your life (family, friends, work, sex)?
2. Do you grow aggressive and disrespectful whenever someone mentions the name "Jeff Finger"?

3. Do you experience rapid mood swings, especially during a Leafs shootout loss?
4. Have you or anyone else close to you ever been injured as a direct result of you throwing something at the TV?
5. Have you ever woken up in the middle of the night, weeping uncontrollably and shouting "Tuukka Rask!" over and over again?
6. Has a romantic partner, friend or relative ever suggested that you just "turn the goddamned game off if it's upsetting you so much"?
7. Have you ever looked up Fred Boimistruck's career scoring stats on the internet?
8. Do you feel mildly aroused whenever someone whispers the words "Holy Mackinaw" in your ear?
9. Have you ever considered looking *truculence* up in the dictionary?
10. Do you experience physical symptoms like anxiety, sweating, nausea, vomiting, insomnia, depression, or irritability whenever Don Cherry says something negative about the Leafs on Coach's Corner?

If you answered "yes" to one or more of these questions, then you may have a Leafs dependency and should seek prompt psychological attention, or at least go for a walk. If you answered "yes" to all of the questions then, dude, you've got a serious problem ... but we've got to admire your commitment.

GAME DAY AFFIRMATION

Today I will reaffirm my commitment to the 12 Steps and accept that in every life a little Vesa Toskala must fall.

GAME 7

Do not let what you cannot do interfere with what you can do.

— John Wooden, legendary NCAA basketball coach and human quote machine

One of the all-time greatest Leafs is almost forgotten now. His name is Cecil "Babe" Dye, and while he might be a big "Huh?" to most fans of the blue and white today, he was the St. Pats' star player, leading them to a Stanley Cup in 1922, and one of the greatest goal scorers the NHL has ever seen.

Dye was a superb athlete who also played halfback for the Toronto Argonauts, and was such a good outfielder that the baseball legend Connie Mack offered him $25,000 — a fortune in those days — to sign with his Philadelphia Athletics. But Dye's first love was hockey, and he knew how to put the puck in the net. In 271 NHL games, he had 201 goals — still one of the all-time best goals-per-game percentages — including an amazing 36 goals in 20 games during the 1917–1918 season.

There were two knocks on Dye: his less-than-stellar skating and his Kesselian lack-of-commitment to defence. Still,

Dye's services were in demand, and one man particularly interested in them was New York Rangers majority owner Col. John S. Hammond.

It was 1926 and Hammond wanted Dye as the centrepiece of the powerhouse team he was putting together. When the St. Pats got into financial difficulty, Hammond ordered his rookie general manager to sign the star at any cost.

But the upstart GM had other ideas and, feeling Dye's liabilities exceeded his assets, defied his boss's decree.

Dye wound up signing with the Rangers' biggest rival, the Chicago Black Hawks, and Hammond fired his GM — a certain Constantine Falkland Cary Smythe — before the first puck even dropped on the 1926–1927 season.

Dye went on to play four more seasons in the NHL, including two years with the Black Hawks and a season with the New York Americans, before finishing his career with a six-game, zero-point stint with the Maple Leafs in 1931. His final point tally probably sums up his career best: 201 goals; 47 assists. A coach's dream or a coach's nightmare? Sometimes one player can be both.

GAME DAY AFFIRMATION

Today I will focus on the things I do well and promise never to pass the puck when I have a clear shot on net.

GAME 8

Luck is what happens when preparation meets opportunity.

— Seneca, Roman playwright and Nero's wingman

As recovering Leafs fans, it's easy to get caught up in the feeling that fate is against us. Fact is, the Leafs never seem to catch a decent break (although, snagging Tomas Kaberle with the 204th pick in the 1996 draft comes pretty close). But it hasn't always been this way. In fact, if it wasn't for a remarkable string of good luck, the Toronto Maple Leafs might not have existed.

The improbable series of events all started with something quite simple. In 1926, after defying that direct order to sign Babe Dye, Conn Smythe was fired by the Rangers. Fuelled by indignation, "the Major" — as everyone called him — returned to Toronto, determined to build a powerhouse hockey team and teach his old bosses a lesson.

He set his sights on purchasing the troubled St. Pats franchise, but there was one big problem: he didn't have the money to do it. The St. Pats had an offer on the table: $200,000 from an American consortium that planned to move the franchise to Philadelphia.

One of the team's directors, though, had a better idea. Jack Bickell, who'd made his fortune in copper and gold mines, owned a big piece of the St. Pats and wanted to see the team stay in Toronto. Bickell contacted Smythe with a proposition: if the Major could come up with $160,000, Bickell would hold on to his shares and together they could take over the hometown team.

Smythe was in. He had a line on some other investors who he knew would be interested, but didn't have a lot of his own money to bring to the table. No money meant no ownership and that didn't sit well with the Major, who was, to put it mildly, a control freak.

Smythe did have some cash, though, including a $10,000 settlement he received from the Rangers after they fired him. But his wife wouldn't let him put it all into a risky business venture like a failing hockey team. She did, however, let him take $2,500 and bet it on a college football game. When the University of Toronto beat McGill, Smythe found himself with $5,000 ... and promptly bet it all on his now-hated Rangers to win a road game in Toronto against the St. Pats.

His team came out on top again, and now with $10,000 in winnings, Smythe had the money he needed to buy his team. And that's how, with a little determination and a lot of luck, the Conn Smythe era began.

GAME DAY AFFIRMATION

Today I will consider Conn Smythe's example and allow myself to sometimes take a chance and risk it all (and if not all, at least $2,500).

GAME 9

> *Nothing happens unless first we dream.*
>
> — Carl Sandburg, poet and semi-professional W.C. Fields impersonator

On Valentine's Day 1927, Conn Smythe finally got what he wanted: control of the Toronto St. Pats. Now he set to remake the team in his own image.

The first thing he did was change the franchise name from the St. Pats to the Maple Leafs. The exact reason for the name change isn't clear — Smythe made a habit of changing his story.

It's a safe bet to assume, however, that his wartime experience played into the choice. Smythe was a legitimate war hero, and he saw action on the worst battlefields the First World War had to offer: Ypres, the Somme, Vimy Ridge, and Passchendaele. He eventually joined the Royal Canadian Air Force and was shot down behind enemy lines and captured. He spent the final year of the war as a German prisoner of war.

Back then, Canadian soldiers fought as part of the British Army, although there were specific Canadian units. As a point of pride, and to distinguish themselves from other Commonwealth countries, our homegrown fighters wore a maple leaf insignia on their uniforms.

"The Maple Leaf, to us, was the badge of courage," Smythe once told a reporter. "The badge that meant home. It was the badge that reminded us all of our exploits and the different difficulties we got into and the different accomplishments we made."

While the name change happened almost immediately, it took Smythe a couple years to get around to changing the team colours. The team played out its first season in green-and-white, with the St. Pats name replaced by a stylized, emerald green maple leaf (if you own one of these sweaters, by the way, it's worth a small fortune: no living person has ever seen one and, amazingly, there isn't even a photo of one).

The Leafs didn't adopt the familiar colours until the 1927–1928 season when players sported plain white sweaters with a blue maple leaf in the middle. It wasn't until the following season that the team first donned the classic Leafs royal blue home sweater with a 48-point white maple leaf insignia on the chest.

Again, Smythe was never clear on why he chose those colours. The official line is that blue represents the Canadian sky, while white stands for omnipresent snow of a northern winter ... but blue and white was also kind of the traditional colours for Toronto teams (think: Argos).

In any case, Smythe's dream had come true. He had his team, and he had control. The entire newborn Leafs Nation waited to see what he would do with it all.

GAME DAY AFFIRMATION

Today I will follow Conn Smythe's example and dare to dream. Then I will wake up and face the grim reality that the Leafs still suck.

GAME 10

*If the doors of perception were cleansed,
everything would appear to man as it is, infinite.*

— William Blake, poet, artist, and confirmed nudist

We've come a long way in a short while. We've recognized that we have a serious Maple Leafs dependency and committed ourselves to facing the problem head on. Now what? Where do we turn to get the help we need?

Fortunately, there is a simple, powerful technique we can all practise that will help us on our road to recovery. It's called mindfulness ... and it's a modern update on ancient self-help practices derived from Zen Buddhist meditation techniques. Mindfulness helps us focus on the present and tap into internal resources — allowing us to take charge of our minds and live richer, fuller, more balanced lives. Think of it as a Brendan Shanahan for your soul.

Why mindfulness for recovering Leafs fans?

Well, the word "mindful" is in the title of this book. So there's that.

Plus, the concepts behind mindfulness are simple to understand, the techniques easy to learn, and the system completely portable (you can practise mindfulness any time, anywhere: in the lunch room on your coffee break; on the subway heading home at night; during the endless pre-game ceremonies at the Leafs' home opener).

Above all, mindfulness is proven effective. Numerous scientific studies have shown mindfulness to help fight major illnesses, reduce symptoms in people with chronic pain, reduce levels of stress and anxiety, alleviate symptoms of depression, and help people deal with compulsive and obsessive behaviours like substance abuse, binge eating, and problem gambling.

Best of all, it's free — or relatively free considering the cover price of this book. Seems like you *can* put a price on happiness: $12.99 ... and that's a bargain.

GAME DAY AFFIRMATION

Today I will be mindful of my thoughts and feelings and appreciate the simple things in life ... like the incredibly reasonable cover price of this book.

GAME 11

He's the man of the hour, at this particular moment.

— Don King, boxing promoter and hair product enthusiast

Here are nine reasons why Major Conn Smythe was cooler than you'll ever be.

1. He was an actual, honest-to-God homesteader. At 17, he ran away from home and started working 150 acres in the middle of the bush, near Cochrane, Ontario. He worked the land for a year, until a fire destroyed his house and he decided his father's home wasn't such a bad place after all.
2. He was a genuine war hero. In February 1917, during a German counterattack in the Somme trenches, Smythe entered the fray, helping free a group of injured Canadian soldiers and killing three Germans in the process. He was awarded the Military Cross for his actions.

3. He spent the last 14 months of the war in a German POW camp. "We played so damned much bridge," he later told a reporter, "that I never played the game again."
4. He was king of the ponies. Smythe was an avid horseman, and his horses won 145 stakes races — only E.P. Taylor's horses won more — including two Queen's Plates.
5. He once was arrested for punching a Bruins fan in the face. I mean, who hasn't wanted to do that? (His excuse: "If I hit anyone, it was only in self-defence.")
6. At age 50, he re-enlisted to fight in the Second World War. He served as a major in the artillery unit and led a unit in the Battle of Normandy where an ammunition truck exploded.
7. He received a Bronze Plaque Award from the Ontario Stone, Sand & Gravel Association. They presented it to him in 1977 for the work that transformed the site of his old gravel business into Smythe Park, "an outstanding recreational area," according to the citation, "with considerable environmental appeal and a distinct asset to the community."
8. He put his money where his (big) mouth was. In 1966, Smythe resigned from the Leafs' board of directors to protest the upcoming heavyweight fight between Muhammad Ali and George Chuvalo. He was

particularly cheesed with Ali's opposition to the Vietnam War. "The Gardens was founded by men who fought for their country," he wrote in his autobiography. "It is no place for those who want to evade conscription."

9. His name is engraved on the Stanley Cup eight times. Your name is engraved on the Cup zero times. Enough said.

GAME DAY AFFIRMATION

Today I will contemplate the legacy of Conn Smythe and remember that no matter how poorly his team may be doing, he remains the coolest owner any sports team has ever had.

GAME 12

> *There are only two mistakes one can make along the road to truth: not going all the way and not starting.*
>
> — The Buddha, famous religious guy and future garden statue model

The new Toronto Maple Leafs debuted on February 17, 1927, to a near-capacity crowd at the Mutual Street Arena (a.k.a. the old Arena Gardens). It was a night of firsts and chock full of the kind of trivia that puts the greatest recovering Leafs fan to the test.

If you can answer one of these questions, it's pretty impressive. More than two, you're a bit of a savant. Three or more and you should seriously consider getting a life.

Questions

1. Who was the first Toronto Maple Leafs coach?
2. Who was the team's first general manager?
3. Who was the first player signed by the Maple Leafs?
4. Who scored the team's first goal?

5. Which was the first team the Leafs faced and what was the game's final score?
6. Who was in the Leafs' net for their debut?

••

Answers

1. Alexander Edward "Porky" Romeril, a standout amateur player, coached the Leafs during the last half of the franchise's inaugural season, while coach-in-waiting Conn Smythe finished his tenure with the University of Toronto men's team. Romeril retired at the end of the season with a 7–5–1 record, and spent the next seven years as an NHL referee.
2. Conn Smythe dug deep and hired himself to be the Leafs' first GM. Smythe remained GM — on paper at least — for the next 30 years.
3. Carl Voss was the first new player signed by the Leafs. The American-born centre/defenceman lasted just over one season with the team, never registering a point.
4. Rookie George "Paddy" Patterson scored the Leafs' first goal on a pass from Bill Brydge at 19:55 of the first period. The Kingston native finished the season with four goals and six assists. Smythe sold him to the

Montreal Canadiens two games into the next season. Patterson went on to a decent NHL career: almost 300 games and 51 goals.
5. Toronto beat the visiting New York Americans 4–1.
6. John Roach — a.k.a. "Little Napoleon" and/or the "Port Perry Woodpecker" — was in goal for the Leafs. Roach had backstopped the St. Pats to their Stanley Cup win in 1922 and was one of seven goalies in NHL history to serve as a team captain. He played two seasons with Toronto before becoming a mainstay in the New York Rangers' net.

GAME DAY AFFIRMATION

Today I will remember that sometimes all you really need to reach your word quota is a little trivia.

GAME 13

> *To live is to suffer; to survive is to find some meaning in the suffering.*
>
> — Friedrich Nietzsche, German philosopher and famous moustache grower

Technically, it isn't true. The Leafs aren't enjoying the longest-standing Cupless streak in the NHL.

The truth is, they have company in their misery. The St. Louis Blues have also gone without a Stanley Cup since the franchise started back in 1967. In fact, the Blues have never won a Cup, nor have the Sabres, Canucks, Sharks, Panthers, Capitals, Jets, Coyotes, Predators, Wild, or Blue Jackets (nor did, for that matter, the Cleveland Barons, Kansas City Scouts, or a long list of other forgotten teams).

So in a way, the Leafs — with their 13 championships — are far better off than most other teams.

Technicalities aside, though, as recovering Leafs fans, we have earned the mantle "long-suffering" honestly and wear it with a kind of pride. We could have given up on our team years ago. But something keeps us coming back.

Perhaps it's because we are innately masochistic: we simply get off on pain. Maybe we suffer from low self-esteem, believing deep down inside that we don't deserve anything better than to be devoted to a crappy hockey team that never seems to go anywhere. It could be that we suffer from deep-rooted psychological needs, stemming from a traumatic childhood. Or perhaps we fear the void — that vast absence that would take over our lives if we no longer had the Leafs to obsess over.

But maybe our biggest weakness is actually our greatest strength. Loyalty, devotion, acceptance — these are positive attributes that every Leafs fan shares, whether we realize it or not. The key is to bring these qualities to the surface and consciously nurture them. This can only come from an understanding that we are not victims of fate, but that being a Leafs fan is an active choice we have made.

We recognize — in fact, embrace — that life isn't fair, but we've made a decision to look past this mundane reality. We should take pride that there is a certain heroism in our devotion to the Leafs.

It's a crazy, deluded, impotent kind of heroism, but heroism nonetheless.

GAME DAY AFFIRMATION

Today I will accept that suffering is part of life and take comfort in the fact that, while the Leafs really suck, at least they're not the Vancouver Canucks.

GAME 14

> *It is the spectator, and not life, that art really mirrors.*
>
> — Oscar Wilde, Irish writer and wallpaper critic

What is a sports fan?

The answer might seem obvious, but, like most things, when you really start to think about it, it's not so simple.

Luckily, psychologists have already turned their pointy heads to the questions, and have come up with some pretty interesting ideas. In fact, according to marketing psychologists Kenneth A. Hunt, Terry Bristol, and R. Edward Bashaw, there are actually five levels of sports fans.

1. Spectators, also known as social fans. These are the people who occasionally get turned on to a sporting event like the Olympics or soccer's World Cup. Social fans' interest in a sport is specific and time-limited, and completely goes away once the event is over. These fans also tend to enjoy the social side of the sport way more

than the sport itself. When the Olympics are on, they'll get together with friends to watch doubles ping-pong or the two-man luge, and the next day talk excitedly about the results with workmates, but they have no sustained interest in the sport.

2. Local fans. These are the people who support a hometown player or team out of a sense of loyalty, duty, or civic pride. But once the focus of attention is removed — the local freestyle swimmer comes home from the Olympics ... the Junior A team moves to another city — the local fan's interest wanes.

3. Devoted fans. These people have an unwavering attachment to a particular team or athlete. They are season-ticket holders and NHL cable-package purchasers, and never miss a game, interview, or highlight reel. They take their team's wins and losses personally, but it takes more than a bad game or losing streak or bad season or even a 50-year drought to deter these folks.

4. Fanatical fans. To say these fans are committed is putting it mildly (in fact, some of them *should* be committed). They have an encyclopaedic knowledge of team facts and figures, follow team developments obsessively, and own all sorts of team gear and paraphernalia — in fact, it's hard to tell where the fan ends and the team begins. Fanatical fans are about as bad as it gets, except for …

5. Dysfunctional fans. In other words, people exactly like you. Actually, probably not. Truly dysfunctional fans — like England's famous, and almost extinct, hooligans — reach a level of obsessiveness and violence that few of us could ever aspire to. This type of fan needs more than a little mindfulness to fix their problem.

GAME DAY AFFIRMATION

Today I will remind myself that being a Leafs fan is a choice and that it is actually humanly possible to like a hockey team without becoming completely obsessed with it. It's called "being normal."

GAME 15

> *Great works are performed not by strength but by perseverance.*
>
> — Samuel Johnson, critic, essayist, and word-definition-thingy writer

Conn Smythe's Toronto Maple Leafs started with a whimper, not a bang.

In the team's first three seasons, the Leafs won fewer than 50 games and missed the playoffs each year.

But there were encouraging signs.

The Leafs' record improved each year, going from dead last in the NHL's five-team Canadian Division in 1927 to fourth in 1928, and to third in 1929.

Meanwhile a number of players established themselves as legitimate stars in the fledgling league. "Ace" Bailey, "Hap" Day, "Shorty" Horne (it was the Golden Age of sports nicknames; the Leafs also boasted "Baldy" Cotton and "Red" Horner) — all of them were getting noticed and helping the home team gain some respectability.

In the 1928–1929 season, the Leafs finished third in their division and actually earned their first playoff berth. They even made it to the second round of the playoffs, beating the Detroit Cougars — remember them? — 7–2 in a single knockout game before losing 2–0 to Smythe's old nemesis, the New York Rangers, in the semifinal.

Despite their budding success, the franchise struggled to make a go financially. The main problem was the old Mutual Street Arena. Built in 1912, the arena was once the largest indoor rink in the country.

By 1930, however, the building was cold; the seats uncomfortable; and with standing capacity capped at almost 8,000, the Mutual Street Arena just wasn't big enough to support a professional hockey team.

The Leafs' losing record didn't help either, and paid attendance hovered around 4,500 people over the first two seasons.

The Major knew he needed to take decisive action and dreamed of building a state-of-the-art facility that would put his team on the map. But there was one thing standing between Smythe and the realization of his vision: a little worldwide financial crisis known as the Great Depression.

GAME DAY AFFIRMATION

Today I will remember that neither Rome nor the Leafs were built in a day, but that even a fallen empire, also like Rome and the Leafs, can be a cash cow if it's marketed properly.

GAME 16

> *Make a list of what is really important to you. Embody it.*
>
> — Jon Kabat-Zinn, mindfulness guru
> and cool last-name owner

As we travel the long road to recovery, it's important to take the time to recognize simple things in life, and to understand that, while problematic, our Leafs addiction isn't all bad. We get a lot of value out of our devotion to this team, and we need to give ourselves permission to appreciate and even celebrate these small things about Leafs fandom that bring us joy.

A great way to start is to make a list of those simple joys that being a Leafs fan brings to you. Here's a little something to get you started …

1. No one expects us to know a lot about wine.
2. Wearing our vintage Miroslav Fryčer jersey and having a random stranger give us the thumbs up on the TTC.
3. Knowing who the Leafs picked in the sixth round of the 2011 draft and why it was a dumb idea.

4. If people want to buy us a birthday present, they know that virtually anything with a Leafs logo on it will do.
5. Passing the old Maple Leaf Gardens and feeling slightly pissed off that it's now a grocery store.
6. Missing the sound of Paul Morris announcing the game's third star on the PA system.
7. Getting all the Leafs in-jokes in the Austin Powers movies.
8. The moment of unspoken camaraderie when we're walking down the street in some foreign country and we see someone else wearing a Maple Leafs ball cap.
9. Eagerly waiting each summer to hear the news that some radio or TV station has, once again, fired Jim Ralph.
10. Muttering "Yolanda" on the TTC, and having fellow passengers look at us in deepest sympathy.

GAME DAY AFFIRMATION

Today I will pay attention to the simple things that bring my life joy and meaning. I will also watch *Austin Powers in Goldmember* because I love that friggin' movie.

GAME 17

> *In order to attain the impossible,*
> *one must attempt the absurd.*
>
> — Miguel de Cervantes, author and
> impossible dream dreamer

The Great Depression hit Canada hard. By 1931, unemployment was rampant, with almost a third of the labour force out of work (two-thirds in some rural areas) and one-fifth of the country receiving some kind of financial aid from the government.

Meanwhile, the gross domestic product — the total value of goods and services produced — plummeted 40 percent or more, and corporate profits, which exceeded $920 million in 1929, turned to a $100 million loss a year later.

It was in the midst of this economic turmoil that Conn Smythe decided to build his dream arena. And in typical Smytheian fashion, he turned the disadvantages he faced into advantages. The Major realized that in a time when money and jobs were scarce, he could offer people a little of the former and a lot of the later. And he could do it all while making the bleak future look a little brighter.

He got the ball rolling by buying an empty lot on the corner of Church and Carlton streets from the T. Eaton Company at the bargain basement price — thanks to a stagnant real estate market — of cash and stock options totalling $350,000.

Then he cut a deal with the workers to pay one-fifth of their normal wages in preferred stock. Not only did this allow Smythe to save money, it gave the workers added incentive to finish the job: the sooner the new arena opened — now dubbed Maple Leaf Gardens — the sooner the value of their stocks would grow.

Smythe broke ground on the arena in May 1930. Seven months, 13,000 tonnes of steel, 13,500 cubic yards of concrete, and 1.5 million bricks later, Maple Leaf Gardens opened its doors. What began as one man's impossible dream was now reality … and would soon become one of the most famous landmarks in the city, if not the country.

GAME DAY AFFIRMATION

Today I will remind myself that impossible is just a state of mind and that anything is possible if you only have a little determination and a lot of preferred stock.

GAME 18

> *Nothing is softer or more flexible than water, yet nothing can resist it.*
>
> — Lao Tzu, philosopher and fortune cookie sage

With a new building to fill, Conn Smythe set his sights on putting together a winning team in Toronto.

After surveying the hockey landscape, Smythe decided that there was one player he wanted more than anyone else: a diminutive, smooth-skating phenom named Francis Michael "King" Clancy.

Clancy was the Ottawa Senators' star player, and considered one of the best defencemen in the league. He was fast, a brilliant stick-handler, and feisty as all get-out despite his 5-foot-7-inch frame. Clancy started a thousand fights, it was said, and won none.

He had patrolled the Ottawa blue line for a decade, having started his pro career at the ripe old age of 18, and along the way, helped the Senators win a pair of Stanley Cups. Clancy is reputed to be the first NHLer to play all six positions in a single game (centre, both wings, both defence spots, and goalie).

It's said to have happened in March 1923, in a Cup match against the Edmonton Eskimos (that's not a misprint!). In those days, Lord Stanley's hardware was awarded to the top professional team in the country and featured a showdown between the top teams from three professional leagues: the NHL, the Pacific Coast Hockey Association (PCHA), and the Western Canada Hockey League (WCHL).

In the third period, Ottawa goalie Clint Benedict was called for tripping, and the ref assessed a penalty that Benedict — as per the rules of the game at the time — had to serve. Clancy grabbed Benedict's goalie stick and gloves and guarded the crease for the entire two minutes.

GAME DAY AFFIRMATION

Today I will strive to follow the lead of King Clancy, to be flexible in the face of adversity and pugnacious in the face of bigger guys, even though it might mean getting my clock cleaned every once in a while.

GAME 19

> *The amount of good luck coming your way depends on your willingness to act.*
>
> — Barbara Sher, self-help guru and lady who said this quote

The Leafs opened the 1931 season in their new home, Maple Leaf Gardens, on November 12 in front of a sold-out crowd of more than 13,000 fans — the highest attendance for a Toronto hockey game to that point.

The game ended in defeat, with the Leafs losing 2–1 to the Chicago Black Hawks on the strength of a tiebreaking goal by Chicago centre Vic Ripley. Despite the loss, it was a big night for Smythe and his team, and was, of course, the scene of a number of historic firsts.

Early in the first period, the Black Hawks' Harold "Mush" March — pride of Silton, Saskatchewan — scored the first goal in the new arena (March would come full circle, dropping the puck for the ceremonial opening face-off at the final game in Maple Leaf Gardens, on February 13, 1999).

Legend-in-the-making Charlie "Big Bomber" Conacher

tied the game late in the second period, becoming the first Leafs player to score in the new building. Unfortunately, however, Ripley's early third-period goal and Chuck Gardiner's stellar goaltending sealed the Leafs' fate.

The night also marked the first game in a Leafs jersey for the team's newly acquired star defenceman. Making good on his promise, Conn Smythe had swung a deal with Ottawa in the off-season for "King" Clancy. And what a deal it was. The cash-strapped Senators got two pedestrian players — Eric Pettinger and Art Smith — plus the unheard-of sum of $35,000.

It was a record, the most any team had paid for an NHL player — and it came about because of the strange combination of determination and blind luck that characterized the way Smythe did business.

The Major knew the Senators wanted a king's ransom for Clancy, but he was a little short of cash himself. He'd got a hot tip on a horse running in the upcoming Coronation Stakes, one of the premier races of the era. At 106–1, Rare Jewell was beyond a long shot to win the race, but the Major placed a $5,000 bet on the nag. To everyone's surprise, Rare Jewell took the race, netting Smythe $14,000 ... which he promptly used to buy the little defenceman with a big heart.

GAME DAY AFFIRMATION

Today I will remember that sometimes to get a proven stud, you have to take a chance on an overlooked filly.

GAME 20

> *Simplicity is making the journey of this life with just baggage enough.*
>
> — Charles Dudley Warner, American essayist and early beard proponent

It's a simple phrase. Four words that summed up the drama, intensity, and passion of what was quickly becoming the most popular sport in the country: "He shoots ... he scores!"

And those words belonged to one man: legendary broadcaster Foster Hewitt.

Hewitt was there at Maple Leaf Gardens on opening night, high above the ice in his famous broadcast booth, dubbed the gondola, calling the game for the General Motors Hockey Broadcast (soon to be renamed *Hockey Night in Canada*) ... and he was still calling the shots 40 years later as the man behind the mic during the Canada-U.S.S.R. Summit Series (infamously mangling the Russian players' names in the process).

A true pioneer in sports broadcasting, Hewitt started off on the sports beat for the *Toronto News* at just 13 years old. By age 20, he was the paper's sports editor but soon left that job for a position with the *Toronto Daily Star*'s fledgling radio station.

The station broadcast only once in a while and Hewitt had to be ready to cover everything from live sports events to religious services. He even read stories for kids at bedtime.

It was while working for the station that Hewitt made hockey history, calling the play-by-play (and providing colour commentary, as it was a one-person operation in those days) for a senior amateur game between teams from Toronto and Kitchener. It was 1922 and Hewitt had just called the first radio hockey broadcast in history.

To say the conditions were primitive is an understatement. Hewitt called the game from an unventilated glass box — which eventually fogged over completely — speaking into a telephone line connected to the studio. Every now and then, the operator would interrupt the action to ask, "What number are you calling, sir?"

The opening night broadcast from the Gardens went ahead despite the protests of a number of Leafs directors, who thought the radio exposure would hurt game attendance. How wrong they were: the show was an instant hit, soon becoming a coast-to-coast institution — Hewitt became the voice of hockey and, to many, the voice of the nation.

GAME DAY AFFIRMATION

Today I will follow the example of the great Hewitt, and focus on the concept of economy of thought and speech. I will also avoid trying to pronounce names like Gennadiy Tsygankov and Viacheslav Solodukhin: I just can't get my tongue around them.

GAME 21

> *I do my job like I breathe — so if I can't breathe I'm in trouble.*
>
> — Karl Lagerfeld, fashion designer and fan fan

Breathe.

It sounds simple enough.

In fact, the average person does it about 20,000 times a day ... 7,300,000 a year.

Despite how often we do it, we don't always do it effectively. When we are stressed, anxious, rushed, or preoccupied with our problems, our breathing becomes rushed and shallow ... and that makes it next to impossible to relax.

Why do we breathe like this? Because most of us live in a constant state of stress. Whether we're rushing to work, trying to jam a quick workout in before we wolf down our dinner, or just freaking out about last night's Leafs game, stress is everywhere.

And, of course, our body's natural reaction to this kind of pressure is what's called the flight or fight response. It harkens back to early in humanity's evolutionary journey, when day-to-day stresses included encounters with sabre-toothed carnivores and snakes the size of subway cars.

When we experience flight or fight, adrenaline courses through our body, causing our heart to race, our blood pressure to rise and our breathing to increase as we ready for the life and death struggle that — these days — almost never comes.

The net result is that we are in a nearly constant state of unnecessary readiness … which makes it almost impossible for us to focus on our mindful recovery.

So, step one on your road to wellness? Take back control of your breathing. It's the easiest, most effective way to relax. Just find a quiet comfortable spot, free of distractions (cell phones off!), close your eyes, and breathe slowly and deliberately.

When you inhale, breathe in all the way, filling your lungs, and hold it for a full second. When you exhale, imagine you are blowing on a candle flame, with enough pressure to make the flame flicker but not go out. Completely empty your lungs, hold for a second, then breathe in again.

Try doing this every time there's a commercial break during the next Leafs game. You'll be surprised how quickly you start to feel calmer, more relaxed, and more focused.

GAME DAY AFFIRMATION

Today I will focus on my breathing, making sure that it's not fast and furious, like a Burke-era rebuild, but measured and steady, like today's ongoing Shanaplan.

GAME 22

> *Some cause happiness wherever they go; others whenever they go.*
>
> — Oscar Wilde, Irish writer and pith master

King Clancy turned out to be well worth Smythe's money.

The feisty Irishman played six full seasons for the Leafs and part of another, retiring in 1936 after 286 games, 52 goals, and 130 points (not to mention a hefty 383 penalty minutes) with the team.

Clancy quickly made the transition to NHL referee, working league games for the next 11 years. Eventually, he returned to the Leafs, taking a job in 1951 as coach of the team's minor league affiliate, the Cincinnati Mohawks. The team did well, winning the Calder Cup Championship in Clancy's first year ... and fell just short of a repeat the following year.

It was the beginning of a long association between Clancy and the Leafs that included a couple of unsuccessful stints as coach, a long-term gig as Smythe's assistant GM — Clancy did mostly public appearances and other PR work — and a long ride into the sunset as Harold Ballard's constant sidekick and platonic soulmate.

But it's Clancy's on-ice achievements and antics that set him apart: from the time New York Rangers defender and part-time pro wrestler Harold Starr lifted Clancy over his head, airplane spun him, then threw him over the boards into the stands, to the time he picked a fight with an unruly Boston Bruins fan (who turned out to be Jack Sharkey, heavyweight boxing champion of the world). Clancy never failed to entertain.

And, oh yeah, he also helped Conn Smythe's biggest dream come true in 1932, playing a big role in the team's 3–0 Stanley Cup Finals win over Smythe's still-hated New York Rangers. What a way to end the Leafs' inaugural season in Maple Leaf Gardens: a new building, a Stanley Cup, and a future full of possibility.

GAME DAY AFFIRMATION

Today I will remember the King, who never failed to put a smile on someone's face. That's it. No sarcastic follow-up. Let's just try being nice for a day.

GAME 23

> *Half the game is mental; the other half is being mental.*
>
> — Jim McKenny, retired Leafs defenceman and one-time pretty boy

Do you have to be literally crazy to be a Leafs fan? Not necessarily, but it helps.

In fact, social psychologists have put in a lot of time trying to figure exactly what — if anything — goes on in the mind of a sports fan.

Turns out, there really is a lot going on. At the heart of every fan's obsession is the abiding sense of belonging — what psychologists call "social connectedness" — that comes with rooting for our favourite team. Social connectedness is actually a critical part of personal happiness and well-being.

The value of sports is that it provides us low-impact, low-risk access to an extensive network of social connections. The mere fact we wear a T-shirt or cap with the Leafs logo on it immediately identifies us as members of a larger group that shares a range of common beliefs, aspirations, memories ... even enemies.

How positive a force is this social connectedness? Well, Daniel Wann, a professor at Murray State University, has turned his research into the psychological well-being of sports fans into a cottage industry — and along the way created something he calls the Team Identification–Social Psychological Health Model.

This model — kind of a working theory — suggests social connections that come from following a local team can make you feel less alone and isolated, increase your self-esteem and openness, and leave you more satisfied with your social life. And the more you identify with your team, the better you probably feel.

Fact is, you don't lose any of these psychological benefits even if the object of your fandom is a perennial loser, like the Leafs. In some ways, the sense of collective futility we feel actually enhances the bonds we have with our fellow Leafs fans.

GAME DAY AFFIRMATION

Today I will accept my need to connect with other humans, especially if those humans are also insanely devoted Leafs fans.

GAME 24

> *A creative man is motivated by the desire to achieve, not by the desire to beat others.*
>
> — Ayn Rand, shallow thinker and proto–Donald Trump wannabe

Before the era of goalie pads the size of tree trunks, and blockers the size of TTC subway doors, there was a goalie named Walter "Turk" Broda who could stop pucks with his mind and short-circuit the Zamboni with a glance.

Okay, this is an exaggeration ... but the man was a monster, leading the blue and white to five Lord Stanleys.

Broda's nickname had nothing to do with the country Turkey. Rather, it was given to him as a kid because his freckle-covered face made him look a little bit like the bird. The name stuck, and who knows how many opposing forwards felt their blood bubble while carving up a turkey on Thanksgiving dinner.

By the way, he took a pause in the middle of his career to fight in this little old thing called the Second World War.

And this is just a footnote in the guy's resumé. Could Turk stop a bullet? Who knows, but it wouldn't be that surprising.

Broda finished his career with an unbelievably low goals against average (1.98) and a slew of Leafs goaltending records that still stand as of 2017: most games played (629); most minutes played (38,168); most wins, regular season (302); most wins, playoffs (101); and most shutouts (62).

The guy could play. And he liked to have fun. And he liked to eat. In fact, he and Coach Smythe had a little kerfuffle over Turk's weight. There came a point when it was either the pancakes or his job, but Turk buckled down and lost enough weight to appease his coach.

GAME DAY AFFIRMATION

Today I will give my all to each moment in the day. Also, I will roast an entire turkey for dinner and savour each bite.

GAME 25

> *Quality is not an act, it is a habit.*
>
> — Aristotle, Greek thinky-guy

Some people are a little like shooting stars. They appear, light up the world, and in an instant, it seems, are gone.

When it comes to recovering Leafs fans, our shooting star is a guy called Irving Wallace "Ace" Bailey. He was there at the very beginning, as part of the transition team from the St. Pats to the Leafs; there when the Leafs played their first home opener at Maple Leaf Gardens; there later that season to score the winning goal at 15:07 of the third period to earn the Leafs their first Stanley Cup in 1932.

For eight seasons, Bailey was a mainstay on the Leafs' forward lines, leading the league in scoring in 1928, making five Stanley Cup Finals appearances, and compiling 114 goals/ 200 points in the course of an all-too-brief career that came to a sudden end in December 1933.

The notoriously gritty Boston Bruins were hosting the youthful Leafs — and the young guns were skating circles around their hosts. Eddie Shore, Boston's All-Star defenceman, was frustrated with the Leafs' hardworking-but-chippy combination of Red Horner, King Clancy, and Ace Bailey.

In the second period, Shore was checked hard into the boards by Clancy and the Bruin turned over the puck. As the Leafs rushed down the ice, Shore shook out the cobwebs and went after the first guy he saw: Bailey. Shore nailed him — got him with his head down — with an open-ice bodycheck. Bailey landed on the ice hard, hitting his head. As the Leafs' team doctor rushed to attend to Bailey, who lay convulsing on the ice, Horner skated up to Shore and slugged him, knocking him senseless. Both Shore and Bailey had to be carried off the ice.

Shore had a headache and a suspension. Bailey was rushed to the hospital where he would spend the next 12 hours battling for his life.

Bailey survived, but his NHL career was finished. A few months later, the Leafs hosted a benefit game to raise funds for Bailey. The game featured the best of the best — Shore being one of them. As the game was about to start, Shore skated over to Ace Bailey and the two shook hands. It seems that all was forgiven by Bailey. But not for Leafs fans, who never forgot the cheap shot that was heard around the hockey world.

GAME DAY AFFIRMATION

Today I will be like Ace Bailey and practise forgiveness. In fact, I'll start by forgiving myself.

GAME 26

There is always tension between the possibilities we aspire to and our wounded memories and past mistakes.

— Sean Brady, Irish clergyman and non-baseball cardinal

As we strive to become more mindful Leafs fans, we've already mastered the power of proper breathing. It's the first step towards learning to relax. The next step is to take conscious control of the stress and tension that rules your body. It's easy to do by practising a simple technique called progressive muscle relaxation.

But before you learn how, it's helpful to learn why. Humans aren't just creatures of habit. We are also creatures of chemicals, and one of the most powerful compounds our bodies produce is a hormone and neurotransmitter called adrenaline. It's the thing behind the flight or fight reaction we have to stressful and anxiety-producing situations.

Unfortunately, modern life is full of little day-to-day stresses (someone cuts us off on the highway; a drunk accosts us on the street; our boss sends us to the minors for getting married without his permission; we get fired from our colour-commentating job). Society doesn't just let us physically express ourselves whenever we encounter a stressful situation: unlike Bob McGill, Al Secord, or Tie Domi, we can't just beat the crap out of everyone who pisses us off.

The result? That powerful adrenaline is bottled up inside, and even though we may not consciously react to stress, our body does. Some people shoulder the burden by tensing up their neck and upper back; some bend over backwards to please and channel the tension to their lower backs; some tense up their mouths, clenching their jaws until their head explodes with a migraine. No matter how we hold our tension, we take it out on some poor muscle group.

That's where progressive muscle relaxation comes on. Think of it as a mental massage for your soul. All you need to do is find a quiet spot to chill for a few moments, then slow your body and mind with a few minutes of deep breathing.

Next, systematically go through all the major muscle groups in your body, first the muscles — tensing them for five seconds as you pay attention to the feeling — then relaxing (as you once again pay attention to the feeling). Start with the feet, move to the calves, then the thighs, then around to the butt, the lower back, the shoulders, the neck and, finally, the mouth and jaw.

Do this for a few minutes every day, and through conscious practice, you'll soon start to notice when and where your muscles are tightening up.

It's a simple but effective exercise to help you be mindful caretakers of your own personal little Maple Leaf Gardens.

GAME DAY AFFIRMATION

Today I will pay attention to what my body is telling me, unless it is telling me not to eat that third maple dip. Then I will just tell my body to shut the hell up.

GAME 27

There is no shortage of fault to be found amid our stars.

— John Green (or in this case, John Blue)

Fast, talented, broad-chested — a natural athlete — Ralph Harvey "Busher" Jackson was destined for the NHL. In his career, Jackson was named to five NHL All-Star teams, was a perennial contender for the league's leading scorer, and held a list of scoring records that wouldn't be broken until a guy named Wayne Gretzky turned pro.

Jackson was only 18 when he joined the Leafs in 1929 and was quickly teamed with Charlie Conacher (also 18) and Joe Primeau (who was 23) to form the Kid Line. They were fast, furious, and effective, quickly establishing themselves as one of the top offensive trios in the NHL.

Jackson lived as fast off the ice as he played on it. He became cocky in his success, and he wanted all of Toronto to enjoy it with him over drinks. But the late nights took their toll: he often found himself in the morning with an empty wallet, a terrible headache, and — most unforgivably of all, in Conn Smthye's book — late for practice.

Smythe showed unusual patience with Jackson, squaring the young upstart's debts and trying to keep him off the booze. But it was all for naught. By 1936, Jackson's scoring declined and the Kid Line was broken up. His time in Toronto ended in 1940 when Smythe included him as part of a five-for-one swap trade for Sweeney Schriner (trivia alert: the first ever Russian-born NHLer).

In 15 NHL seasons, Jackson scored 259 goals and added 246 assists, won a Stanley Cup, made a few All-Star appearances — even led the league in scoring in 1932. But his career was over by the time he turned 33. By then, he was a serious alcoholic, his wife had left him, and he was almost broke (it's said he sold broken hockey sticks the Leafs gave him to earn money). Worn out and alone, he died at age 55 — a sad ending for a fondly remembered star from the Leafs' good old days.

GAME DAY AFFIRMATION

Today I will remind myself to go easy on the Leafs players, remembering that, deep down, they're just regular guys like you and me.

GAME 28

What do you think of your team's execution? — I'm all for it.

— John McKay, former Tampa Bay Buccaneers coach,
summing up what every coach feels at some point

Clarence "Happy" Day was a pretty good Leafs player, who turned out to be a pretty great coach (259 wins, five Stanley Cup victories).

Hap Day was with the Leafs from the very beginning: he was captain of the St. Pats when the Major took over the team. He played 13 seasons with the Leafs — including 11 seasons as captain, second only to George Armstrong — and after a single season with the Rangers, finished his career with 213 points in 637 NHL games. Not bad for a stay-at-home defender.

Day started coaching the West Toronto Nationals, a local junior team, while he was still playing for the Leafs, and proved himself an adept bench boss by leading the Nats to a national Memorial Cup Championship in 1936. Two years later, he retired from pro hockey and, after a couple years as an NHL ref, ended up behind the bench in the big league, coaching his old team, the Leafs.

Day proved to be an ardent taskmaster as a head coach. He demanded accountability on the defensive end and worked players to the bone during practice to improve their conditioning. His iron-fist approach paid off, as the Leafs responded with a 28–14–6 record — good for second overall in the NHL. Although they lost in the Stanley Cup semifinals to the Bruins, the Leafs took it all the following season in a memorable Stanley Cup Finals comeback against the Detroit Red Wings in 1942.

An astute coach, Day also understood how his own boss worked. Day was never late for work, arriving at Maple Leaf Gardens early every morning, even before Conn Smythe. And after a phone call to Greenwich, England, he'd set all the clocks around the arena ... precise: just how the Major liked it. Day also had a phone line installed on the home team bench so he could talk directly to Smythe if the occasion called for it.

He wasn't exactly Smythe's lapdog, but he was certainly his hatchet man, doing, in Smythe's own words, everything he "couldn't do: fire people, bench them, live always on what a man could do today, not on what he had done a few years ago."

Day finished his tenure as Leafs coach in 1950, but stayed on as assistant general manager (and essentially GM in 1955, although Smythe still held the job on paper).

And did this tremendous loyalty pay off?

Yes and no. In the end, Day wound up a fairly wealthy man, with seven Stanley Cups to his credit as both a player and as a coach/manager. But the ending was acrimonious and typically Leafian: after the Leafs finished fifth out of six teams and failed to make the playoffs, Smythe told the press that he wasn't sure if Day was available to return for another season. This was news to Day, who promptly quit the team, and barely spoke to his long-time boss, business associate, and supposed friend ever again.

GAME DAY AFFIRMATION

Today I will remember that in Leafs Nation, loyalty is not necessarily rewarded … and in the long run, if I want happy days, I might have to watch the reruns on TV.

GAME 29

It ain't over 'til it's over.

— Yogi Berra, legendary New York Yankees catcher
or maybe Lenny Kravitz

As recovering Leafs fans, we have learned to take the good with the bad. In fact, we have learned to cling like death to those moments of good just to endure the long, long moments of bad we've experienced.

And when it comes to great moments, none are better than the 1942 playoff series.

The Leafs finished the season with a great record (27–18–3, good for second place overall), two players in the top 10 for points (Syl Apps and Gordie Drillon, with 41 points each), and perennial All-Star Turk Broda in net.

A good season was nice, but the Leafs had gone ten years without a Cup — an amateur drought by today's standards, but a drought nevertheless.

The Leafs started well, beating the first-place New Rangers four games to two in the semifinals. But then the

Leafs ran into the red-hot Detroit Red Wings, and things came to a crashing halt.

The Wings had rolled over the Montreal Canadiens and Boston Bruins in the first two playoff rounds, and kept the momentum going, beating the Leafs in the first three games of the best-of-seven Stanley Cup Finals.

Facing elimination, Hap Day pulled out all the stops for Game 4, reading a letter from a 14-year-old fan, imploring the team not to give up. For added emphasis, he benched Drillon and "Bucko" McDonald, two-thirds of his top line, and brought in rookies Don Metz and Ernie Dickens to take their spots.

Something worked. The Leafs squeaked by in Game 4, with Syl Apps tying the score with six minutes to go in the game, and Metz — making Day seem like a genius — popping in the game winner just minutes later.

Game 5 was a romp, with Metz scoring a hat trick and adding a couple of helpers to lead the Leafs to a 9–3 drubbing of the Wings. Game 6 was another toughie, with the Wings peppering the Leafs' goal with shots. But netminder Turk Broda stood on his head, earning a shutout in a 3–0 win to tie the series.

Game 7 was played in Toronto in front of 16,218 fans — a Canadian record for a hockey game. Syd Howe — no relation to Gordie — opened the scoring early in the second period, but Sweeney Schriner buried one on the power play early in the third to tie it and fourth-line centre Pete Langelle scored the go-ahead goal three minutes later. The Leafs hung on to win the game 3–1, earning a third Stanley Cup for the franchise and making sports history along the way.

Only four times in major team sports has a team come back from being down by three games in a playoff series. The first team — and the only to do it in a league final series — was the 1942 Toronto Maple Leafs.

GAME DAY AFFIRMATION

Today I will remind myself that moments are to be cherished. I will also make a mental note to get my kids to write a letter to Mike Babcock, reminding him how badly we all want a damned Stanley Cup.

GAME 30

> *The strong do what they have to do and the weak accept what they have to accept.*
>
> — Thucydides, Greek general, political theorist, and possible souvlaki inventor

While recovering Leafs addicts will remember Syl Apps as a Leafs legend, he was a multi-talented man who came in sixth in pole vaulting at the 1936 Berlin Olympics and went on to serve 12 years as the Progressive Conservative Member of the Legislative Assembly for Kingston.

Apps was also a perfect gentleman of the highest order — winning the NHL's Lady Byng Trophy for sportsmanship in 1942 — who once returned a paycheque because he had been sidelined with an injury. In fact, he was so nice, people worried early on if he was too sensitive for the NHL. Boy, did he show them up.

Apps is up there in the Leafs' records books: 432 points in 423 games — good for seventeenth on the team all-time scorers list. He also finished his career with a whopping 56 penalty minutes (11 minutes fewer than what L.A. enforcer Randy Holt once earned in a single game).

Apps led the Leafs to three Stanley Cups, captaining the Leafs for six seasons — also taking a pause in between to fight in the Second World War. He went out in style, scoring a hat trick in his final regular season game. We can finally put the old adage to rest. As Apps proves, sometimes even nice guys finish first.

GAME DAY AFFIRMATION

Today I will remember the virtue of good manners and honesty, as embodied by Syl Apps. I will not, however, return a paycheque just because I took a sick day. That's taking the whole nice-guy thing too far.

GAME 31

Of course there is no formula for success except, perhaps, an unconditional acceptance of life and what it brings.

— Arthur Rubinstein, renowned pianist and Chopin fanboy

If there is one certainty in life, it's that nothing is ever certain.

Meteorologists and palm readers try their best to predict how crappy our morning commutes or seventh marriages will be, general managers assure us that our latest draft pick is destined to become the league's next marketable superstar, doctors advise us that eating poutine for every meal will make us fat (okay, so that one is probably true) ...

The truth is, the future is unpredictable, and the past is irreparable.

This is a scary thought. It is frightening for things to happen differently than how we think they should. We want to believe we are in good hands. We want to believe that our players are immune to wrist and shoulder and ankle and knee injuries. We want to believe we will snap out of that lengthy playoff drought. We want to believe we will never trade away another first-round pick unless something better than a Tom Kurvers will come of it.

Being a recovering Leafs fan is often a balancing act of hope and agony, facilitated by our brain's magical capacity to concoct fantasy scenarios: the if-onlys, the shoulda couldas, the what-will-be's, the imagine-ifs …

However, as practising students of mindfulness, we must learn to embrace acceptance as if it were Mats Sundin playing for the Vancouver Canucks.

Acceptance is a mindset. It is an alignment of oneself to the reality of a current situation. That doesn't mean you have to like the current situation as it is.

It also doesn't mean you can change the situation. But it does mean you have to accept everything that has led up the situation, and welcome whatever may come of it.

GAME DAY AFFIRMATION

Today I will allow myself to accept the Leafs — Shanaplan or not — as they are right now and allow myself to feel fine about it.

GAME 32

Knowledge can be communicated, but not wisdom.

— Hermann Hesse, author and
guy with fun name to say

Conn Smythe was a visionary; he took risks and made things happen. In the fall of 1947 — after a Cup win — Smythe essentially traded an entire starting lineup to the Chicago Black Hawks for the stud centre Max Bentley.

Having grown up on a farm in Saskatchewan, Bentley credited his deadly backhand to milking cows — yes, milking cows. Bentley, the youngest of six hockey boys, learned quickly that "if they can't hit you, they can't hurt you" — and he brought that frame of mind to the ice.

Max and his brother Doug were Chicago's go-to two, but that was about all the Black Hawks had. With no depth, and having missed the playoffs in 1947, Chicago was desperate. Smythe knew that the Hawks needed players; he also knew that he wanted to add another all-star centre to his team to go along with the Sly Apps/Ted Kennedy one-two punch.

So on November 2, Smythe shocked the hockey world by sending former rookies of the year Gus Bodnar and Gaye Stewart, their linemate Ernie Dickens, along with winger Bud Poile and defender Bob Goldham — an entire starting lineup — to Chicago for Bentley and Cy Thomas (the Welsh-born footnote in a blockbuster deal).

Smythe's gamble paid off. In Bentley's first two seasons with the Leafs, the team won back-to-back Cups — for the first three-peat in NHL history — and added another Cup two years later. The Major proved once again that he was the best of the best.

GAME DAY AFFIRMATION

Today I will remember the Major's example and accept that no matter how smart I am, I sometimes have to bet it all if I want to win big.

GAME 33

> *The difference between ordinary and extraordinary is that little extra.*
>
> — Jimmy Johnson, legendary football coach and euphemism-enhancement shill

If there was ever anyone who let his play on the ice speak for him, it was Leafs legend Ted "Teeder" Kennedy. Quiet, unassuming, talented as all get out, Kennedy was the epitome of the strong silent type — starring for the Leafs for 14 seasons without ever losing perspective.

Kennedy was called up to the Leafs for a two-game tryout in 1943 after a stellar season with the Port Coburn Senior Men's team, where he scored 23 goals in 23 games. The following season, Kennedy made the Leafs for good, turning heads with a stellar first-year performance that included 49 points in 49 games (although Calder Cup honours for rookie of the year went to Kennedy's teammate, Gus Bodnar, who tallied 62 points in 50 games).

The next season, Kennedy led the Leafs in scoring with 54

points in 49 games, adding a team-leading nine playoff points on the way to his first of five Stanley Cups with the team.

By 1949, he was regarded as one of the league's elite players, and Hap Day named him the Leafs captain. Day's faith was rewarded, as Kennedy once again led Leafs playoff scorers during another Stanley Cup campaign — and along the way, Kennedy became the youngest player in league history to captain a Cup-winning team.

Despite his on-ice achievements — youngest player to score 100 goals, a Hart Trophy in 1955 (the last Leaf to win league MVP honours) — Kennedy was never a flashy personality. Although he appeared in six All-Star games, he was selected only as a Second Team All-Star three times, and was never honoured with a First Team All-Star selection. It was a huge oversight, but as the Leafs then-assistant general manager Frank Selke once said, as a player Kennedy "lacked one thing — colour."

Still, Kennedy's legacy lives on. He retired in 1957 with 250 goals and 360 assists — and remains to this day in the Leafs' top 10 for goals, assists, and points — while his 60 playoff points is a record for any Leaf. Most of all, he remained a quiet, unassuming leader to his very last playing day.

GAME DAY AFFIRMATION

Today I will remember Ted Kennedy's example and eschew the need for external validation (who needs those damn All-Star team selections anyway) and focus on who I am as a person.

GAME 34

> *The greatest test of courage on earth is to bear defeat without losing heart.*
>
> — Robert Green Ingersoll, lawyer and free thinker, whatever the hell that is

Forget about 50 years without a Stanley Cup. As Ted Kennedy's story reminds us ("Teeder" was the last Leafs player to win the Hart Trophy as league MVP — that's over a 60-year drought, folks), the Leafs have been woeful when it comes to taking home the hardware.

In fact, the last Leafs player to win a major award — Alexander Mogilny — didn't even want the thing. Back in 2003, Mogilny refused to pick up his Lady Byng Memorial Trophy for sportsmanship, calling it the consolation prize he did not need. Mogilny didn't even show up for the awards ceremony, leaving coach Pat Quinn to accept the Lady Byng for the enigmatic Russian.

As for other awards? Let's test your knowledge. Can you name the last Leafs player to win each award, and the year he won it?

1. Hart Memorial Trophy — League MVP
2. Art Ross Trophy — NHL Scoring Leader
3. Maurice Richard Trophy — NHL Goals Leader
4. Vezina Trophy — Top Goalie
5. Calder Memorial Trophy — Top Rookie
6. James Norris Memorial Trophy — Top Defender
7. Frank J. Selke Memorial Trophy — Top Defensive Forward
8. Jack Adams Award — Coach of the Year

• •

Answers

1. You already knew that Ted Kennedy won the Hart in 1955, but did you know that he earned it on the strength of 10 goals and 42 assists, good for 11th overall in NHL scoring? In truth, Kennedy was probably given the award out of guilt. He was coming to the end of a distinguished career and had actually retired at the start of the season before Conn Smythe talked him into playing one more year. The Hart selection was the NHL's way of saying sorry for all those missed All-Star games.
2. The correct answer is no one. Since the award was introduced in 1947, no Leaf has led the NHL in scoring.

In fact, the last Maple Leaf to do so was Gordie Drillon in 1938, on the strength of 52 points in 48 games.
3. Another bust. The NHL introduced the Richard Trophy in 1999, 53 years after the last Leaf led the NHL in goal scoring (Gaye Stewart, with 37 goals in 1945–1946).
4. Johnny Bower and Terry Sawchuk shared the Vezina in 1964–1965, back in the day when the trophy was given to the team whose goaltender(s) allowed the fewest goals. Leafs goalies have come close a couple times since then, with Curtis Joseph the bridesmaid in both 1999 and 2000.
5. Brit Selby — remember him? — was rookie of the year in 1966 with 27 points in 61 games, the lowest point total for any Calder winner since 1938 … when the NHL season was 48 games long. Wendel Clark came close to winning a Calder in 1985, finishing third in voting (Gary Suter took home the hardware).
6. Another bust. No Maple Leaf has ever earned NHL best defenceman honours since the award's inception in 1953–1954. Börje Salming came close in 1977 and 1980, but close, as we all know, only counts in horseshoes and hand grenades.
7. Is this really a major award? Seemingly invented so Bob Gainey could get an award each year, the Leafs'

Doug Gilmour actually won this in living memory, racking up 127 points and a +32 in 1993.
8. Pat Burns was coach of the year in 1993; he'd already won it once, in 1989, with Montreal, and would win it again in 1998 with Boston.

GAME DAY AFFIRMATION

I focus on the present moment because the past is so, so, so far away.

GAME 35

> *The person who rides a donkey
> cannot avoid smelling its farts.*
>
> — African proverb

As recovering Leafs fans, we have learned to take the good with the bad. In fact, we've been riding this donkey for so long, it's probably more accurate to say that we've learned to take the bad with the worse.

It seems that for Leafs Nation, even the greatest successes have a foul odour to them.

Consider the story of Frank Selke, a legendary general manager with the Montreal Canadiens, nine-time Stanley Cup winner, and member of the Hockey Hall of Fame. Known for being a pioneer of defensive-style hockey, Selke's name lives on — the Frank J. Selke Memorial Trophy is awarded each year to the NHL's top defensive forward.

Selke actually started his pro hockey career with the Leafs. In 1929, after a successful career in junior hockey —

earning two Memorial Cups — the Maple Leafs' Board of Directors hired Selke as the top-assistant manager of the Leafs franchise. In 1939, the board made Selke acting general manager while Conn Smythe was overseas, fighting in the First World War.

Selke and Smythe were both headstrong men, and actually built up a strong animosity over the years — starting in 1943 when Selke traded up-and-coming defenceman Frank Eddolls to the Montreal Canadiens for the rights to a relatively unknown player named Ted Kennedy. Of course, Kennedy would go on to be a Leafs legend, but at the time, the Major hated the trade. He was high on young Eddolls and pissed that Selke made the deal without consulting him. Some say you could hear Smythe cursing from across the Atlantic.

After Smythe's return from the war, their relationship disintegrated further: first when Smythe retook the helm from Selke, and then when Selke refused to support Smythe's bid for club president. However, Selke stayed with the team until 1946, helping them earn three Stanley Cups along the way. But here's where things get a little ... malodorous. In 1945, the Leafs defeated the Detroit Red Wings in seven games, and, as is tradition, Lord Stanley's trophy was subsequently etched with the names of all the team players, coaches, and management.

Selke's name is right there with the others, with one curious notation. Hoping to save space (or maybe at the prompting of Conn Smythe, who was not above petty game playing) the engraver abbreviated Selke's title — Assistant Manager — to "ass man."

So there it is: Selke's success slightly tainted by a lazy engraver ... proving that in Leafsland nothing's ever simple. No ifs, ands, or *butts*.

GAME DAY AFFIRMATION

Today I will give myself permission to plug my nose and enjoy the world around me.

GAME 36

The trouble with having an open mind, of course, is that people will insist on coming along and trying to put things in it.

— Terry Pratchett, fantasy writer and famous hat wearer

It's best to keep an open mind, just not literally.

Along with being present-focused, openness is one of the keys to mindfulness. However, while being present is more about calibrating where your attention lies, openness is about shifting your mindset.

So, what does it mean to be open?

The best place to start is by understanding what it means to be closed to experience. As a recovering Leafs fan, being closed is easy to grasp. It means shutting ourselves off from unpleasant experiences — a shootout loss or, back in the day, a Ken Dryden press conference — which in turn, provoke unpleasant emotions. We accept these unsavoury events as just the way things are — and in turn we may feel helpless. Being closed to experience means having a pre-conceived notion of how a thing is or what its outcome will be.

We may think: "Sure we're on a two-game home-stand winning streak, but we'll get back to losing once we're on the road. We're the Leafs." We tell ourselves that we can't handle watching another crappy game or disappointing season. However, sentiments like that are just the way our brains have learned to cope with negativity. In fact, we are quite capable of dealing with anything the Leafs can throw at us, if we simply adjust our lens of perception.

Being open involves cultivating an attitude that is dynamic — a belief system that isn't limited, a mindset that eschews the onerous weight of established tradition (which kind of sounds like Harold Ballard's approach to running the Leafs).

Openness is about freeing our minds from the limits of past perceptions, seeing things with fresh eyes, like a child looking at a strange new flower for the very first time.

Even the worst thing the Leafs have ever done — bringing Imlach back for another go, alienating Dave Keon, trading Russ Courtnall for John Kordic — can be looked at with fresh eyes and an open mind.

Maybe Imlach needed to return to Toronto to complete his spiritual growth.

Maybe Keon needed to learn his own lessons about openness and non-attachment.

Maybe Gord Stellick had his head so far up his own ass he was experiencing some kind of profound mystical awakening that imbued the stupidity of that trade with some kind of higher purpose.

You never really know.

GAME DAY AFFIRMATION

Today I will empty my mind so that no matter what is thrown my way, I will embrace it openly.

GAME 37

> *Whoever said, "It's not whether you win or lose that counts," probably lost.*
>
> — Martina Navratilova, first-rate tennis player, second-rate dancer

We've already talked about the importance of social connectedness in the psychological makeup of a sports fan, but what about those lapses we all have, those moments when we decide, once and for all, to give up on our beloved team? What do psychologists have to say about the fickle nature of sports fandom?

Quite a lot, actually, and most of it is related to something called the social identity theory. Developed by a British-based psychologist, Henri Tajfel, and his student John Turner (no, not *that* John Turner), the theory basically says that we often build up our own self-esteem by identifying with the success of someone — or something — else.

In the case of Leafs fans, not only do we identify with our team, but we actually exaggerate the importance of the team to make ourselves feel more important. The technical term for this phenomenon is BIRGing — Basking In Reflected Glory — with "reflected" being the key. We don't earn any of the glory ourselves; we merely bask in our team's success.

BIRGing has its downside. For one thing, it promotes an us-versus-them mentality — Leafs are great, Habs suck — which can lead to fan fights and, in extreme cases, violent group outbursts like the 2011 Stanley Cup riots in Vancouver.

The opposite of BIRGing? Why, CORFing of course. As recovering Leafs fans, we're CORFing — Cutting Off from Reflected Failure — whenever we go through our annual ritual of rejecting the Maple Leafs.

True Leafs fans — the most pathetic cases, like us — are not true CORFers, though. While we might temporarily turn our backs on the team, we always come back eventually. But rather than criticize ourselves for our weakness, let's move forward mindfully, embracing our Inner BIRG, accepting it and harnessing its hidden strength to help us grow and flourish.

GAME DAY AFFIRMATION

Today I will give myself without judgment or condemnation, and forgive myself for those inherent weaknesses that make me human and for my unrelenting devotion to the Leafs, which is, frankly, just plain stupid.

GAME 38

> *From nobody to upstart. From upstart to contender.*
> *From contender to winner. From winner to champion.*
> *From champion to dynasty.*

— Pat Riley, legendary NBA coach and Conn Smythe wannabe

As recovering Leafs fans, we are aware that during some point in the universe's history, the Maple Leafs were the team to beat in the NHL.

In fact, during most of the 1930s the Leafs were the NHL's version of the National Football League's bridesmaid Buffalo Bills: always in it, never quite good enough. Bookended between championships in 1932 and 1942, the Leafs appeared in six more Stanley Cup Finals, falling a win (or two or three) short in 1933, 1935, 1936, 1938, 1939, and 1940.

But the 1940s — they belonged to the Maple Leafs. With an iconic general manager in Conn Smythe, a passionate, precise coach in Hap Day, and a cast of All-Star and future Hall of Fame players, the Leafs were *the* league powerhouse. In nine years, between 1942 and 1951, the Leafs won the Cup six times.

Like most successes, it didn't come easy. Pro hockey took a backseat when the Second World War broke out, and the slew of players, including Turk Broda, Syl Apps, and Sweeny Schriner — not to mention the Major himself — went overseas to fight. But the Leafs' supporting players were up to the challenge, and the underdog Buds beat the highly favoured Detroit Red Wings in the 1945 Stanley Cup Finals.

The rest, as they say, is Leafs history. Starting in 1947, and with rookies and role players picking up the slack, the Leafs won three Cups back-to-back-to-back for the first three-peat in NHL history.

They took a slight break, letting the Red Wings have a Cup in 1950 (after all, the roster was full of gentlemen like Syl Apps and Ted Kennedy). But the Leafs were back the next year, bringing another Stanley Cup back to Toronto.

For a full decade, the Leafs were feared, dominating the ice, scoreboard, and, basically, the NHL. They were an intimidating force, featuring more than a dozen future Hall of Famers, earning a slew of NHL records and six Stanley Cups — and those special years will never be forgotten by Leafs fans as the first Maple Leafs Dynasty.

GAME DAY AFFIRMATION

Today I will remind myself to take a nap as soon as we start losing, so I can at least dream about the Leafs' glory days.

GAME 39

I take things like honour and loyalty seriously. It's more important to me than any materialistic thing or any fame I could have.

— Lloyd Banks, American hip-hop artist and, you know, yo!

It might be hard to believe, but the Toronto Maple Leafs are the undisputed champs when it comes to players in the Hockey Hall of Fame. If you count players from the Blueshirts, Arenas, and St. Pats, there are 62 franchise players in the Hall, along with 15 men in the Builders category (including owners, GMs, coaches, and broadcasters).

The list of Toronto Maple Leafs Hall of Fame players is long and distinguished, with names like Syl Apps, Johnny Bower, Dave Keon, Darryl Sittler, and … Fernie Flaman?

Fernie Flaman? Who the hell is that?

Ferdinand Charles Carl "Fernie" Flaman was, in fact, the premier defensive defender of the 1940s and 1950s. While he spent most of his long NHL career — 20 years, 910 games — patrolling the blue line for the Boston Bruins, he played four seasons with the Leafs, helping them win a Stanley Cup in 1951.

And speaking of surprising Leafs Hall of Famers, did you know that a Boston Bruins goaltending legend is also included on the list of Leafs inductees? Gerry "Cheesey" Cheevers — he of the terrifying, scar-crossed mask — was actually Leafs property in the early 1960s, toiling mostly in the minors ... although he did get in a couple games with the big team in the 1961–1962 season.

In any case, here is the full list of Leafs players (minus the non-Leaf franchise inductees) in the Hall of Fame, along with the year of their induction.

Glenn Anderson (2008)
Syl Apps (1961)
George Armstrong (1975)
Ace Bailey (1975)
Andy Bathgate (1978)
Ed Belfour (2011)
Max Bentley (1966)
Leo Joseph Boivin (1986)
Johnny Bower (1976)
Turk Broda (1967)
Gerry Cheevers (1985)
King Clancy (1958)
Charlie Conacher (1961)

Hap Day (1961)
Gordie Drillon (1975)
Dick Duff (2006)
Cecil Henry "Babe" Dye (1970)
Fernie Flaman (1990)
Ron Francis (2007)
Grant Fuhr (2003)
Mike Gartner (2001)
Doug Gilmour (2011)
George Hainsworth (1961)
Red Horner (1965)
Tim Horton (1977)

Phil Housley (2015)
Syd Howe (1965)
Busher Jackson (1971)
Red Kelly (1971)
Ted Kennedy (1966)
Dave Keon (1986)
Brian Leetch (2009)
Eric Lindros (2016)
Harry Lumley (1980)
Frank Mahovlich (1981)
Lanny McDonald (1992)
Dickie Moore (1974)
Larry Murphy (2004)
Joe Nieuwendyk (2011)
Frank Nighbor (1947)
Bert Olmstead (1985)

Bernie Parent (1984)
Pierre Pilote (1975)
Jacques Plante (1978)
Babe Pratt (1966)
Joe Primeau (1966)
Marcel Pronovost (1978)
Bob Pulford (1991)
Börje Salming (1996)
Terry Sawchuk (1971)
Sweeney Schriner (1962)
Darryl Sittler (1989)
Allan Stanley (1981)
Mats Sundin (2012)
Norm Ullman (1982)
Harry Watson (1994)

GAME DAY AFFIRMATION

Today I will take the name Fernie Flaman as my personal mantra, and in mindful contemplation, repeat "Fernie Flaman" over and over and over again until I achieve a state of higher consciousness (or until the game ends, whichever comes first).

GAME 40

It is better to light a candle than curse the darkness.

— Eleanor Roosevelt, former first lady and distant cousin of FDR

Every sport has its curses, and Leafs Nation is home to one of the most famous hockey curses of them all (and no, we're not talking about Harold Ballard and his legacy).

It all began in Game 5 of the 1951 Stanley Cup Final between the Leafs and the Montreal Canadiens. Toronto was up three games to one in the series — although the results didn't reflect the closeness of the competition. Every game had gone into overtime.

The Leafs were behind late in the game until a Tod Sloan shot tied things up with 32 seconds left. Less than three minutes into overtime, stalwart defender Bill Barilko — never an offensive powerhouse — broke in from the blue line. He took a Howie Meeker pass and, just as he was being tripped, banged the puck past the Habs' keeper, Gerry McNeil.

Sadly, the championship glow did not last long. Four months later Barilko and his dentist, Henry Hudson, went on a fishing trip in northern Ontario. Something went horribly wrong: the plane went missing. A massive search found nothing. The plane had no doubt crashed; Barilko and Hudson had certainly died.

The Leafs didn't win another Cup during the 1950s. Rumour was that the team was cursed and they'd never win again until Barilko's body was found.

In 1962, the curse came to an end. The Leafs defeated the Black Hawks in six games to take their 10th Stanley Cup. Seven weeks later, the wreckage of Barilko's plane was found in the bush near Cochrane, Ontario — a slightly inverted ending to Canada's most famous curse.

GAME DAY AFFIRMATION:

Today I will remember Bill Barilko and remind myself that it's not about how often you win but how awesome you are when you do.

GAME 41

> *No person was ever honoured for what he received.*
> *Honour has been the reward for what he gave.*
>
> — Calvin Coolidge, U.S. president and answer
> to the trivia question, Who is Calvin Coolidge?

Bill Barilko's sweater was the last Leafs number to be retired for almost 65 years.

After number 5 was raised to the Gardens' rafters, the Leafs established a policy: numbers would only be retired in those rare instances when an active, prominent player was seriously injured or died.

It made sense to the ever-thrifty Major Smythe: there are only so many sweater-friendly numbers available to a team. You can't just take them out of circulation willy-nilly. Just ask the Montreal Canadiens. The team has retired 15 numbers between Jacques Plante's number 1 and Patrick Roy's number 33. That takes a lot of options off the table.

Instead of retired numbers, the Leafs had a tradition of honoured numbers — celebrating a player's achievements without taking the number out of circulation. There were 10 honoured numbers in the Leafs' pantheon, three of which — Wendel Clark's 17, Mats Sundin's 13, and Doug Gilmour's 93 — have never been worn since their fêted owners retired.

The honoured number policy changed dramatically, however, at the start of the Leafs centennial season. At the home opener, the Leafs raised all 10 honoured numbers one more time — this time retiring them forever. And along the way, they added Dave Keon's number 14 for good measure.

Seven honoured numbers were worn by other players after their owners hung up the skates. Can you match the honoured number with the last Leafs player to wear it?

#1 — (Johnny Bower, Turk Broda) A. Cody Franson
#4 — (Hap Day, Red Kelly) B. Colby Armstrong
#7 — (King Clancy, Tim Horton) C. Andrew Raycroft
#9 — (Charlie Conacher, Ted Kennedy) D. Mike Peca
#10 — (Syl Apps, George Armstrong) E. Ian White
#21 — (Börje Salming) F. James van Riemsdyk
#27 — (Frank Mahovlich, Darryl Sittler) G. Alex Steen

GAME 41

Answers

#1 — C. (Andrew Raycroft)
#4 — A. (Cody Franson)
#7 — E. (Ian White)
#9 — B. (Colby Armstrong)
#10 — G. (Alex Steen)
#21 — F. (James van Riemsdyk)
#27 — D. (Mike Peca)

GAME DAY AFFIRMATION

Today I will give myself a bonus point for smugly pointing out that even though number 6 was retired, Ron Ellis wore the number — at Bailey's personal request — for part of his career. Congrats! Now, how about getting that life you've been talking about?

GAME 42

Never waste a minute thinking about people you don't like.

— Dwight D. Eisenhower, U.S. president and
Alfred E. Newman look-alike

Being in the moment.

We've all heard that expression — and it's a core principle of mindfulness — but what does it actually mean?

It's simple really. Most of us spend our time either dwelling in the past or thinking about the future. Maybe we are reliving the Leafs' glory years (back-to-back-to-back Cup wins in the early 1960s), dwelling on a bad trade (Alex Steen and Carlo Colaiacovo for Lee Stempniak? Come on!), feeling preoccupied with a petty argument with a loved one, or just looking forward to the day (in the dim and distant future) when the Leafs will rise again …

It doesn't matter. We have become habituated to this now-or-then thinking, which takes our focus away from the actual moment we are living in.

The problem is that we have become slaves to time, forgetting that the concept of time is, in itself, just a made-up thing: an arbitrary measurement that helps watchmakers and word-a-day calendar publishers pay the bills, but really has no power over us.

Of course, it's easy enough to say "live in the present," but how do you go about doing that? Luckily, as Leafs fans we actually have a great model to follow. We know when we're into watching a game — we pay attention to each pass, each body check, and every missed offside call. We react immediately to the things that are unfolding before us, yelling at the ref when he misses an obvious trip, jumping to our feet and cheering when our boys slip one past the opposing goalie.

Being in the game, 100 percent engaged — that's what being in the moment is all about.

GAME DAY AFFIRMATION

Today I will be in the moment, focusing on the game as it unfolds rather than on the team that once was or could be again.

GAME 43

> *You can't cross the sea merely by standing and staring at the water.*
>
> — Rabindranath Tagore, Bengali mystic, poet, and owner of the coolest name in this book

George "Chief" Armstrong: simply put, one of the greatest players to ever don a Leafs uniform.

He started with the Leafs as a 20-year-old, with a two-game cup of coffee in 1949. Two years later, Smythe called him up again. He played 20 games with the Leafs that year, and never looked back.

Six years later, the Leafs named Armstrong captain — a position he held for a team record of 13 years. Quite an honour for a man who came from humble beginnings, born into an Irish-Algonquin family just outside Sudbury, where his father worked in the nickel mines.

Never having the gentlest of hands, he earned a reputation as a dependable workhorse and capitalized on opportunities. And capitalize he did — assisting on the goal that sealed the Leafs' 1962 Stanley Cup win against the Black Hawks ... and scoring the last goal in the 1967 Leafs Stanley Cup Final (and, need we remind you, the last Stanley Cup–winning goal any Leafs player has ever scored).

After the Cup win, Armstrong decided to hang up his skates ... only to change his mind and return the following season. In fact, he announced his retirement five times — surely that must be a record — but didn't actually bow out until 1971 when he took a front office position with the Leafs. Seems like, despite his best efforts, he just couldn't say no to the game — something recovering Leaf fans, and their wealthy therapists, understand all too well.

He finished his career with four Stanley Cups, seven All-Star appearances, the record for most games in a Leafs uniform (1,298, which includes the playoffs), 713 points (ranking him fifth on the Leafs all-time points list), 296 goals (tied for sixth on the all-time goals list with Frank Mahovlich), and 417 assists (fifth, all time) — proving in the end that hard work and tenacity pay off, just like they say in all those stupid sports clichés.

GAME DAY AFFIRMATION

Today I will consider the example of George Armstrong, focusing not just on the quantity of my days but on the quality of each moment. I will also announce my retirement, then change my mind, just for shits and giggles.

GAME 44

> *Beauty is not the goal of competitive sports, but high-level sports are a prime venue for the expression of beauty.*
>
> — David Foster Wallace, famous author and noted footnoter

If you think you're too short to play sports, look no further than Johnny Bower, only a meagre 5 foot 9, but a hearty 170 pounds. Like "Turk" before him, the guy was a straight-up stud, leading the Leafs to four Cups, including a succession of three in a row between 1961 and 1964. He was also a nice guy; during his first year, he changed his last name from Kiskzan to Bower because the latter was easier to pronounce for sportswriters. It kind of rolls off the tongue, doesn't it? Bower.

But even "Bower" pales in comparison to his nickname, "The China Wall," which tells you all you need to know about his goaltending acumen. And like Broda before him, he had a stint in the Second World War. In fact, he was only 15 years old at the time, having lied about his age in order to enlist. Maybe that's where he honed his reflexes. Maybe that's where he grew his heart.

He maintained a solid GAA of 2.51 in the regular season and 2.47 in the playoffs, also racking up 37 regular season shutouts and five playoff shutouts. But those statistics cover up how long his career actually was. He played until he was 45, and almost suited up at 55 when the Leafs signed him as a backup on a one-day contract when the regulars, Mike Palmateer and Paul Harrison, were feeling under the weather. This is a hefty career for a guy who grew up so poor as a kid that he had to use an old mattress for pads and tree branches for a makeshift stick.

In 2014, the Leafs organization included him in Legends Row, recognizing him as one of the 10 best players in Leafs history.

GAME DAY AFFIRMATION

Today I will remember that there was once a time, eons ago, when the Leafs won three Cups in a row. This will make the reality that the Leafs now suck sting so much more. No pain, no gain!

GAME 45

A rose by any other name would smell as sweet.

— Juliet Capulet, the original heartbreaker

Teeder. Just a simple contraction of Ted Kennedy's given name. Pretty boring as far as sports nicknames go. Often in hockey, the perfect nickname is a tricky thing to acquire. It must be earned: moulded by quality play, cherished by fans, and echoed by broadcasters, formed using an ideal brew of creative wordplay, timing, and dumb luck.

The Leafs have never been short of great nicknames. Can you identify each Leafs player by his nickname?

Nickname

1. The Big M
2. The Milkman
3. Weed
4. Shrimp
5. Radar
6. Jolly Jack
7. The Albanian Assassin

Answers

1. Frank Mahovlich, legendary Leafs forward, given the nickname to distinguish him from his pretty good player-brother, Pete "The Little M" Mahovlich.
2. Claire Alexander — who mostly had a reputation as a standout amateur player — got the nickname because, before he was a pro, he actually worked as a milkman for some time.
3. Mats Sundin. Okay, so this one doesn't really have a meaning, but it is funny isn't it? Doug Gilmour thought it up for Sundin and it sort of just stuck.
4. Lloyd Andrews allegedly loved to eat seafood, plus he was undersized for a winger.
5. Al Arbour. A member of the Stanley Cup–winning 1963–1964 Leafs, he was dubbed Radar for his incredible on-ice awareness.
6. Jack Adams. Given the moniker for the reason that he always seemed to be happy on the ice, no matter what was going on.
7. Tie Domi. He was an enforcer on the ice. The nickname speaks for itself.

GAME DAY AFFIRMATION

Today I will describe my team's play with words more creative than the word "sucky." I will also strive to find better names to call my players than "Some nobody" or "What's-his-face."

GAME 46

> *When the going gets weird, the weird turn pro.*
>
> — Hunter S. Thompson, some junkie

Punch Imlach: known for his fiery temper, brimmed hats, and his ability to win games at any cost.

Imlach joined the Leafs in 1958 as co-general manager — along with King Clancy — answering to a seven-member administrative committee headed by the Major's son, Stafford Smythe. Imlach was not happy with the situation, and gave the team an ultimatum: make him the boss or cut him loose.

In November, he got his wish (the boss part, not the stuff about being cut loose): he was named Leafs GM — just the third in the team's 40-year history — and immediately set to work. By the end of the first week as GM, he fired head coach Billy Reay. By the end of his second week, he'd hired a new coach — himself — keeping the title of GM as well.

It probably didn't hurt Punch's coaching prowess that he'd enlisted in the Second World War, where he'd had his first opportunity to coach a military team near Cornwall, Ontario. He brought a don't-question-me attitude with him from the army team directly to the NHL, which elicited the most from his players (although it occasionally rubbed them the wrong way). Feisty, probably to a fault, Punch didn't shy away from challenges, even the seemingly impossible challenge we know as the Maple Leafs.

And at that point, things were looking pretty bad for the Leafs. The team was in the NHL basement, even as Imlach publicly boasted that he would take the Leafs to the playoffs.

It seemed an impossible feat. But GM Imlach added a core of veteran players — Carl Brewer, Allan Stanley, Larry Regan, and Gerry Ehman — to the team, giving Coach Imlach enough horsepower to get his team on a late-season tear. The Leafs squeaked into the playoffs, one point ahead of New York's foundering Rangers, and the Imlach legend was born.

Imlach was almost as famous for his off-ice quirks as his team's on-ice performance. He had a passel of superstitions that included an obsession with the numbers 7 and 11, a fear of two-dollar bills, and the infamous 1967 playoff run, when Imlach wore the same ugly sports jacket game after game, believing that if he took it off, the team would lose.

Even the Major — no slouch himself when it came to eccentricities and control-freakedness — considered his GM/coach a bit of a nutcase. But as long as Imlach was winning on the ice, Smythe didn't mind what he did.

And win they did. Imlach led the Leafs to their second Stanley Cup three-peat, with Championships in 1962, 1963, and 1964. And the Leafs remained a powerhouse throughout most of the 1960s.

Quirky, polarizing *and*, with 414 total wins, the most successful coach in the Leafs' history — that's Punch Imlach in a nutshell, which is, by the way, where he probably belonged.

GAME DAY AFFIRMATION

Today I will think of Punch Imlach and remind myself that every once in a while, it's fun to go a little batshit crazy.

GAME 47

> *Winners do what losers don't want to do.*
>
> — Gary Busey, sometimes actor and last guy on earth you should take advice from

Tim Horton. His name is synonymous with hockey — and coffee — in this country.

But before he was famous for brewing the beloved beverage that singlehandedly keeps you awake during morning office meetings, he was better known for his play on the ice.

Horton was a standout on the Leafs blue line for 18 seasons — and although he wasn't huge by any means, standing barely 5 feet 9 inches, he is still regarded as one of the strongest players to ever lace 'em up. Mr. Hockey, Gordie Howe, called Horton the strongest man he had ever played against, while Bobby "The Golden Jet" Hull — no shrinking violet himself — once said that there were players in the NHL "you had to fear because they were vicious and would slam you into the boards from behind ... but you respected Tim Horton because he didn't need *that* type of intimidation. He used his tremendous strength and talent to keep you in check."

Ready and reliable on the ice (not unlike his namesake double-doubles), Horton still holds the Leafs records for most consecutive games played — never missing one of 486 consecutive games, from 1961 and 1968. He was also the first Leaf to reach 1,000 games.

Horton had a powerful slap shot. And he was no slouch when it came to the offensive side of the game either. He scored 40 points in 74 games in the 1968–1969 season, and his 16 points in the 1962 playoffs stood as a Leafs record for defencemen until 1994 (when Dave Ellett scored 18 points in 18 games).

Horton left the Leafs in 1969, and after stints with the New York Rangers and Pittsburgh Penguins, wound up back with Punch Imlach, who'd become general manager of the expansion Buffalo Sabres.

At 42, Horton seemed to find his second wind with the Sabres, and helped stabilize their young defence ... until tragedy struck. In the early morning of February 21, 1974, he was driving back to Buffalo after a game in Toronto, apparently driving quite fast, when he lost control of his car. The car rolled a number of times and Horton was thrown from the vehicle. He died a short time later.

It was an untimely end for a man who left an enduring mark on the Leafs, finishing with more than 1,400 games played, 500-plus points, four Stanley Cups, and six All-Star game appearances — earning him a place on the Leafs Legends Row.

GAME DAY AFFIRMATION

Today I will focus on the value of consistency (the Tim-Horton-Iron-Man-streak consistency, that is, and not the Leafs-go-cupless-a-half-century kind).

GAME 48

> *Namaste.*
>
> — Kelly, the lady who tries to sell us
> Echinacea root at the farmers' market

In meditation, the connection between the mind and the body is a powerful and ancient force. Bliss can only be achieved when the mind and the body are working in synchronous symbiotic synthesis.

As sports fans, we know how important it is to keep a pure, healthy physique. But sometimes it's easier said than done — the headaches from lost games, the sore throats from frenzied chants, the broken fists from accidental drunken altercations with lippy Flames fans.... You get the picture. All of these things interfere with our pursuit of bodily serenity. Luckily, there is a common spiritual discipline that we can practise in order to keep our anatomy in tip-top shape: yoga.

Grab those mats! Here is a list of Leafs-inspired yoga poses that we can use to achieve sound body and mind:

- *Maple Tree Pose:* Stand up as straight as you can. Keep your shoulders back and chest out. Put your Leafs jersey on. Try to keep your head held high.

- *The China Wall Pose:* Widen your stance. Bend your knees so that you are in a nice powerful position. Put your hands out in front of you, palms facing outward. An excellent pose for wannabe goalies.

- *Loser Pose:* Face your body to the floor in a fetal position. Keep your knees bent with shins on the floor. Stretch your head forward, touch your forehead to the ground, swallow your sadness. Highly beneficial for headache relief or if you just want to be alone for a while.

- *Hockey Night in Canada Pose:* Sit your butt cheeks comfortably on your favourite seat. Feel your feet firmly on the floor. Extend your arm to use the remote controller. Turn the television on. Keep your eyes fixed on the game for the next two to three hours. You may take breaks if you need to pee.

- *The Tiger Pose:* Bring your feet shoulder-width apart. Reach your hands high into the air, then slowly bend at your hips. Bring your hands down and touch the floor. Maintains great upper body mobility for activities such as throwing punches or hip-checking.

GAME DAY AFFIRMATION

Today I will stretch it out and get in touch with my inner self ... or at least try touching my toes.

GAME 49

Progress is impossible without change, and those who cannot change their minds cannot change anything.

— George Bernard Shaw, Irish playwright and famous fussbucket

The early 1960s were a time of great change: the Cold War, the popularization of the mini skirt, the rise of the Beatles — but most importantly, Red Kelly's move from defence to centre.

Leonard "Red" Kelly came to the Leafs late in the 1959–1960 season from the Detroit Red Wings ... after personally scuttling a deal that would have sent him to the New York Rangers.

When he arrived at Maple Leaf Gardens, he was an All-Star defenceman with four Stanley Cups under his belt. But Imlach knew that Kelly was a graceful puckhandler and adept passer who had occasionally played centre for the Wings. Imlach asked Kelly to play centre full time, and stuck him between superstar-in-the-making Frank Mahovlich and the ever-dependable Bob Nevin. Just like that, one of the deadliest offensive lines in hockey was born.

When Kelly made his Leafs debut at the Gardens on February 10, 1960, it was standing room only. The crowd chanted his nickname over and over again until he stepped onto the ice to take — to everyone's surprise — the opening face-off. The subsequent roar — Kelly later admitted — made the hair on the back of his neck stand on end.

Imlach's calculated gamble paid off. The change immediately paid dividends. In Kelly's first full season with the Leafs, Mahovlich had 48 goals and 84 points in 70 games, while Kelly scored 20 goals or more in each of the next three seasons. In his seven-plus seasons with the Buds, Kelly won four Stanley Cups, finishing his career with 823 points. Not bad for a guy who played most of his career on defence.

GAME DAY AFFIRMATION

Today I will remember that change is possible. I will imagine "Red" scolding me each time I think the future is fixed.

GAME 50

> *I had only one superstition. I made sure to touch all the bases when I hit a home run.*
>
> — Babe Ruth, baseball's early home run king and semi-edible candy bar

Punch Imlach wasn't the only one with seemingly bizarre superstitions.

Former Leaf Joe Nieuwendyk ate two pieces of toast and peanut butter before every game. Current Leafs honcho Brendan Shanahan wore his lucky junior hockey shoulder pads for the first 10 years of his NHL career, and always listened to Madonna before each game. Jocelyn Thibault, who tended net for more than 586 NHL games, poured water on his head exactly six-and-a-half minutes before game time. Black Hawks legend Stan Mikita smoked a cigarette between periods, and always threw the butt over his left shoulder before hitting the ice again.

Hockey's full of them. Weirdo superstitions. And, as recovering Leafs fans, we are not immune to the odd quirk. In April 2002, Maple Leaf Sport & Entertainment, Ltd., asked Leafs fans to send in their game rituals. They were only too happy to comply, and sent 2,500 responses, sharing their therapeutic rituals after decades of trauma. One Leafs fan made sure she parked at the same spot and walked through the same gate each Leafs game; another dressed the newborn in a Leafs sleeper; while a third (the poor soul) ordered a pizza with 13 toppings to honour number 13, Mats Sundin. Unfortunately, we have to admit, given the Leafs track record, none of these rituals were particularly successful.

Sports fans in general frequently subject themselves to a curious psychological phenomenon called superstitious conditioning. It was B.F. Skinner, dean of American behavioural psychology, who first identified the effect through experiments on pigeons. Skinner starved the birds, getting them down to a svelte 75 percent of their normal body weight, then stuck them in a cage.

Skinner was trying to study operant conditioning, which generally meant modifying behaviour with a reward or punishment, and in this specific case meant using the reward of food pellets to train the birds to perform a task (for example, pecking a red square). What Skinner observed, though, was that the pigeons often incorporated accidental moves — like turning in a circle or lifting their head — into their reward routine.

Skinner called these associated but inconsequential moves a "sort of superstition," and likened them to the rituals developed by athletes and fans.

Wear your Lucky Leafs underwear at every home opener? Superstitious conditioning.

Never bathe on game days? Superstitious conditioning.

Get up to grab a beer on a power play so the Leafs score? Superstitious conditioning (or maybe you're just thirsty).

In any case, as Skinner proved, there's very little difference between a Leafs fan and a pigeon. But you probably knew that already.

GAME DAY AFFIRMATION

Today I will eschew all forms of superstition, cross my heart and hope to die.

GAME 51

> *The only difference between this and Custer's last stand was that Custer didn't have to look at the tape afterward.*
>
> — Terry Crisp, former Tampa Bay Lightning coach, after his team lost a game 10–0

Today, even amid all our sucking, there are glimpses of hope, like the occasional winning streak (usually at the end of the year, with the season all but lost) or a promising rookie who makes his mark in the minors (only to get traded when the next general manager takes over). But back in 1964, the Leafs were the opposite. In the midst of monumental crappiness — including a team record 11–0 loss to the worst club in the league — they did pretty darn well overall.

It was January 18, 1964, and the first-place Buds were playing the last-place Boston Bruins in what should have been a meaningless game.

Boston scored in the first minute and were up 6–0 at the end of the first period.

Historic comeback? Think again.

When all was said and done, Bruins Andy Hebenton and Dean Prentice each had hat tricks — on the way to the 11–0 romp.

Leafs had backup Don Simmons in net — he actually had a pretty good NHL career, and had played an important part in the Leafs' 1962 Stanley Cup win. And it wasn't entirely his fault the Leafs stank the joint out. The team had become complacent, and the big loss was a bigger wake-up call.

Following the embarrassing blowout, Punch Imlach decided to shake things up, trading four up-and-comers — Dick Duff, Bob Nevin, Rod Seiling, and Arnie Brown — to the New York Rangers for right-winger Andy Bathgate and centre Don McKenney — both adept but aging All-Stars.

The trade was controversial: the pundits felt Imlach had mortgaged the future. But once again, the gamble paid off. McKenney ran up 15 points in the 15 games remaining in the regular season, while Bathgate had 18 points and added another nine in 14 playoff games, including scoring the game-winning goal that brought the Leafs their third straight Stanley Cup.

GAME DAY AFFIRMATION

Today I will remember that every cloud has a silver lining, even if that cloud lasts for 50 years and the silver lining is getting to draft Auston Matthews first overall.

GAME 52

> *Pain is temporary. Quitting lasts forever.*
>
> — Lance Armstrong, cyclist and guy who definitely does not take steroids

Bobby "Boomer" Baun was never an offensive juggernaut. He never had more than 20 points in any one of his 17 seasons, and over the course of 964 NHL games he racked up a grand total of 224 points. Still, he was a hardworking stay-at-home defenceman … and managed to score one of the biggest goals in Leafs history when it counted the most.

It was game six of the 1963–1964 Stanley Cup Final, with the Leafs trailing in the series 3–2. It had been a tight series all along: Toronto took the first game 3–2, with Detroit taking the next two games by identical 4–3 scores. The Leafs bounced back, taking game four 4–2, but Detroit tied the series up, squeaking by the Leafs 2–1 in Game 5.

The stage was set for Game 6, which was as tight as all the others. By the end of regulation time, the teams were deadlocked at three goals apiece.

Along the way, Baun had been injured sliding to block a Gordie Howe slap shot. When the shot struck Baun's ankle, it sounded like a cannon going off, and the Leafs blueliner lay on the ice writhing in pain. He was unable to get up of his own accord and had to be carried off by the training staff on a stretcher.

It seemed like he was done for good. But the Leafs' doctor shot him up with Novocain to kill the pain, and there he was, on the bench, at the start of the overtime frame.

Barely two minutes into the extra period, Baun intercepted a Detroit clearing attempt and took a slap shot in the general direction of the Red Wings' legendary goaltender Terry Sawchuk. Along the way, the puck deflected off defenceman Bill Gadsby and then skimmed over Terry Sawchuk, who had slid out to protect his net.

The Leafs won the game, and tied the series to force Game 7.

It was an amazing performance that earned Baun a permanent place in Leafs lore ...

GAME DAY AFFIRMATION

Today I will remember that pain is part of the process, and remind myself that, given all the pain Leafs fans have endured for the last half century, we have a lot of gain coming our way.

GAME 53

> *If nothing else works, a total pig-headed unwillingness to look facts in the face will see us through.*
>
> — Blackadder, TV character and time-travelling philosopher

When Punch Imlach predicted that the 1958 version of the Leafs he inherited would make the playoffs, no one believed him. The team was mired in last place, with little hope of advancing out of the basement let alone all the way to the playoffs.

But make the playoffs they did, and in part because of a little proto-mindfulness technique that Imlach embraced, called the power of positive thinking. Based on the book of the same name by pastor-turned-amateur-psychologist Norman Vincent Peale, who endorsed a kind of self-brainwashing technique that maintained that people can achieve success simply by repeating to themselves positive self-statements.

"Change your thoughts and you change your world," Peale once wrote. "Believe in yourself! Have faith in your abilities! Without a humble but reasonable confidence in your own powers you cannot be successful or happy."

Peale's work was immensely popular at the time, selling a couple million copies in the years after its release in 1952 (although not the 20 million Peale would later claim), and turning its author into a major celebrity.

But success came at a price. Psychologists criticized the book for its outlandish and unsubstantiated therapeutic claims; for its anecdotal approach, which was hard to verify if not a tad made-uppy-sounding; and for Peale's secretive use of self-hypnosis techniques. Still ... it's hard to criticize someone who's encouraging people to say nice things to themselves and who almost single-handedly invented the modern self-help movement (for which the authors of this little tome say "thanks" and "ka-ching!").

Plus, Peale's book has a prominent place in Leafs lore. Legend has it that Imlach mandated his players to read it and the team did actually turn things around (Mike Babcock, take note: forcing your players to read a certain self-help book could pay dividends). And while Imlach didn't necessarily embrace the principal to positivity himself — he was known to be a negative and divisive force around the dressing room — it's hard to argue with success, no matter how modest.

GAME DAY AFFIRMATION

Today I will take Imlach's teachings to heart and say nice things to myself: I'm a beautiful person. I'm a valuable human being. And despite my relentless addiction to the Maple Leafs, I am capable of making good choices every once in a while.

GAME 54

The speed of the leader is the speed of the gang.

— Mary Kay Ash, business leader and makeup pro

Before the freefalling plunge into suckiness after 1967, our rosters in the 1960s were stacked with talent ... and perhaps no Leafs players was ever so bursting with raw talent as Dave Keon.

Wee Davie (Keon was only 5 foot 5, and weighed 163 pounds soaking wet) made his debut in the NHL in 1960, at the start of the Leafs' glorious decade. It's fair to say that he started with a bang — winning the Calder Memorial Trophy as the league's top rookie on the strength of a 20-goal, 45-point campaign.

It was obvious from the start that Keon was the complete package: fast as greased lightning, elite offensive skills, defensively responsible, and the epitome of sportsmanship. He won the Lady Byng Trophy for gentlemanly play twice, in 1962 and 1963 — earning just a single penalty in each of those seasons. In fact, in almost 1,300 NHL games, Keon received only 117 penalty minutes (and a fifth of those penalties came in a single season, after his return to the NHL following a six-year stint in the World Hockey Association).

During the Glory Days, Punch Imlach relied on Keon to shut down the opposing team's most dangerous centres. With the luxury of having the older and more experienced Red Kelly as the centre on the top line, Imlach had the opportunity to bring Keon on slowly, allowing the player to reach his potential, culminating in the 1967 Stanley Cup–winning run, when Keon had three goals and eight points in 12 playoff games, shut down opposing stars, and earned the Conn Smythe Trophy as the playoffs' most valuable player along the way.

It was the last of four Cups Keon won with the Leafs, and although he remained with the team for another eight seasons, tensions between the Leafs star and team owner Harold Ballard grew more and more strained. Things came to a head when Ballard publicly criticized Keon's leadership ability — a deliberate and unsupportable insult designed to try to get Keon to waive his no-trade clause. That wasn't the end of Keon's Ballardian woes. While Keon could theoretically sign with another NHL team, that team would also have to financially compensate the Leafs with an amount

Ballard set unreasonably high. As a result, no one was willing to take on the 35-year-old Keon, who was, for all intents and purposes, prevented from continuing his career in the NHL. (While Ballard was petty, self-centred, and possibly the physical incarnation of evil, we have to admit that he knew how to smite his enemies.)

Keon jumped to the WHA, and harboured ill feelings toward the Leafs that lasted until 2016, when he finally agreed to allow the team to honour him with a statue on Legends Row. Still, Keon remains a Leafs legend — to this day, he's second in goals scored (389), third in points (916), and uppermost in every fan's heart.

GAME DAY AFFIRMATION

Today, in honour of Dave Keon, I will do all of my normal activities super fast. I will run to the bathroom during commercial breaks with extra speed. I will press the button on the remote so fast my finger will appear a blur. When I talk, my words will barely be comprehensible at their flying force. (But I will still eat slowly. Heartburn is real.)

GAME 55

Frank was a gentleman in a cruel sport.

— George "Punch" Imlach, Leafs coach
and master de-motivator

As recovering Leafs fans, it's hard to live in the moment. This was never more evident than on one night back in November 1967. The Leafs had just trounced the Canadiens 5–0, led by the stellar play of the team's offensive dynamo, Frank Mahovlich. He'd had a great night, with a goal and two assists — and was a force every time he stepped on the ice.

But that wasn't good enough for Leafs fans. Egged on by Punch Imlach — who'd been attacking his top player openly in the press — the boobirds were out in full force. They jeered the Big M at every turn, even booing him when he scored a goal. And at the end of the night, as he skated across the ice to acknowledge his selection as the game's First Star player, they booed some more.

The next day, as the team boarded a train for Detroit, Mahovlich disappeared. The Leafs' perennial leading scorer — still the highest-scoring left-winger in team history — had suffered a nervous breakdown and had checked into a hospital. He wasn't the first victim of the Leafs' pressure cooker and he wouldn't be the last. But he might have been the best.

Frank never really recovered his Leafs mojo. He was traded to Detroit the next year and would go on to star for the Red Wings and the Montreal Canadiens, finishing his career with more than 1,300 NHL games (he'd add another 250 or so in the World Hockey Association), 1,221 points, 14 All-Star Game appearances, and six Stanley Cups ... proving that, no matter what the pundits and Punch Imlach might think, nice guys like Syl Apps, Ted Kennedy, *and* Frank Mahovlich don't always finish last.

GAME DAY AFFIRMATION

Today I will focus on the moment and suppress the critical voice of my inner Imlach in order to allow the full Mahovlich inside me to shine.

GAME 56

> *No artist is ahead of his time. He is his time;*
> *it is just that others are behind the times.*
>
> — Martha Graham, the Wayne Gretzky of modern dance

Mike "Shakey" Walton was a curious figure in Leafs history. A transitional figure, a modern, professional player stuck in an outdated, old-school system.

Walton came to the Leafs as a highly touted prospect, who knew — with 41 goals and 92 points in his final season in juniors — how to put the puck in the net. He went on to win back-to-back Rookie of the Year awards (in 1965 playing for the Tulsa Oilers of the Central Professional Hockey League, and a year later, playing for the American Hockey League's Rochester Americans).

And though it took him a while to crack Punch Imlach's veteran-laden Leafs lineup, when he did, he did it with style. He scored seven goals — almost all of them on the power play — during the Leafs 1967 run to the Cup, and the following season he outscored the likes of George Armstrong, Ron Ellis, and Dave Keon to lead the Leafs in scoring.

Despite his success, Walton never quite clicked with the Leafs powers that be. Imlach never warmed to him — the coach/GM constantly ragged on Walton about his "long" hair and was not enamoured with Walton's agent, Alan Eagleson, the driving force behind the fledgling NHL Players' Association.

Walton married Conn Smythe's granddaughter, who also happened to be niece to Stafford Smythe, de facto boss of the Toronto Maple Leafs.

Given the pressure he was under (and his unfamiliarity with proper breathing, guided relaxation, and other mindfulness techniques), it's no wonder Walton got stressed to the max. He was examined by an NHL-appointed psychiatrist, who diagnosed depression and recommended, believe it or not, a change of scenery.

Imlach was happy to accommodate, sending Walton to the Boston Bruins in a three-way deal that landed the future Hall of Fame goalie Bernie Parent in Toronto and sent another future Hall inductee, Rick MacLeish, to the Philadelphia Flyers.

Walton had a pretty good year in Boston, playing with his junior teammate Bobby Orr and racking up 28 goals and 28 assists in 76 games. He hung around pro hockey for another decade, playing with the Vancouver Canucks, the

St. Louis Blues, and the Chicago Black Hawks, and doing a three-season tour of duty with the World Hockey Association's Minnesota Fighting Saints, where he played once again with his old Leafs teammate Dave Keon.

Walton finished his NHL career with 201 goals and 448 points in 588 games. Not bad for a man ahead of his time.

GAME DAY AFFIRMATION

Today I will celebrate the things that make me different, recognizing that being an original sometimes rubs traditional thinkers the wrong way. That's their problem, not mine. I will also go to Shakey's in Bloor West Village for a plate of suicide chicken wings just because they're so dang good!

GAME 57

Just play. Have fun. Enjoy the game.

— Michael Jordan, NBA legend and guy who ought to know

When the Leafs dealt Walton, they got a lot in return; they just didn't realize it. Centrepiece to the trade was a promising young goalie named Bernie Parent, who went on to have a stellar career ... sadly, with the Philadelphia Flyers.

But let's not dwell on that. Instead, let's have some fun and test your Leafs trivia knowledge (even recovering Leafs fans have to burn off steam sometimes).

Think you know your Leafs? Match the cornerstone players in each of these famous — and infamous swaps. Who's the main player the Leafs gave up, and who was the coveted prize they got in return?

GAME 57

1. Tuukka Rask
2. Larry Murphy
3. Francois Beauchemin
4. Greg Paternyn
5. A first- and second-round pick in the 2007 draft and a fourth-rounder in 2009
6. Mike Eastwood
7. Mike Johnson
8. Gary Leeman
9. Niklas Hagman

A. Mikhail Grabovski
B. Tie Domi
C. Dion Phaneuf
D. Andrew Raycroft
E. Darcy Tucker
F. Doug Gilmour
G. $$$
H. Vesa Toskala and Mark Bell
I. Joffrey Lupu

• •

Answers

1 — D (from the Boston Bruins); 2 — G (Winnipeg Jets); 3 — I (Anaheim Ducks — plus the Leafs got Jake Gardiner!); 4 — A (Montreal Canadiens); 5 — H (St. Louis Blues); 6 — B (Detroit Red Wings); 7 — D (Tampa Bay Lightning); 8 — F (Calgary Flames, as part of a 10-player deal); 9 — C (Flames again … thanks guys!).

GAME DAY AFFIRMATION

Today I will trade in work boots for some runners … and give myself permission to have fun (regardless of the final score).

GAME 58

> *Why should I put a bunch of Cadillacs on the ice, when I can sell out with a bunch of Volkswagens?*
>
> — Harold Ballard, hockey team owner and architect of Maple Leaf doom

October 13, 1971. That's the day the world changed for Leafs Nation. On that day, Stafford Smythe — son of legendary Leafs founder Conn Smythe — passed away, leaving Harold Ballard sole owner of Maple Leaf Gardens Ltd.

Ballard joined the Leafs in 1957, as part of the Stafford-Smythe-led "Silver Seven" — the management team that oversaw all Maple Leafs business (including the hiring of Punch Imlach). Four years later, Ballard and Smythe the younger (along with newspaper owner John Bassett) bought most of Conn Smythe's Leafs shares, and the group installed Ballard as team vice-president.

When Ballard took on the team seven years later, he quickly morphed into a kind of anti-Conn, taking everything the Major stood for — integrity, honour, courage, loyalty —

and turning it on its head. And while Ballard's on-ice antics were legion (losing Bernie Parent to the World Hockey Association, alienating Dave Keon, humiliating Roger Neilson, pushing out stars Lanny McDonald and Darryl Sittler), they almost paled in comparison to his off-ice antics.

Almost.

Off ice, Ballard feuded with almost everyone he could, including:

- The NHL — In the mid-1970s, when the league ordered teams to put players names on the backs of their jerseys, Ballard (eventually) complied, but he put the names in white on the white home jerseys and in blue on the blue away ones.
- Journalists — He called Barbara Frum, respected host of CBC Radio's widely successful news show *As It Happens* "a joke" during an on-air interview.
- His family — He publicly described his daughter as a "reptile" and once cancelled a peewee game at Maple Leaf Gardens because he heard his grandson was playing in it.
- Fans — Aside from the product he put on the ice, Ballard also used to take a cut of scalped tickets (from tickets he provided at cost to his favourite scalpers).
- The Beatles — During the Fab Four's 1966 Toronto show, Ballard cranked the heat and turned off all the water fountains at the gardens, just to make life

unpleasant for Fab Four fans (and sell them soft drinks at three times the normal price). The previous year, Ballard had sold tickets to two Beatles shows even though he knew full well they were only going to play one.
- The Queen — During a 1971 renovation of the Gardens, Ballard had workers remove a portrait of Queen Elizabeth II to make room for more seats. When people complained, Ballard defended himself, saying that the Queen "doesn't pay me, I pay her. Besides, what the hell position can a queen play?"
- And, most of all, Leafs tradition — During the same renovation (and jealous of Conn Smythe's on-ice successes) Ballard sold off all Stanley Cup banners to the highest bidder. Later, he had workers throw Foster Hewitt's famous gondola into the incinerator, over the protests of the Hockey Hall of Fame, just because he could.

As recovering Leafs fans, we must recognize that all of us are suffering from PTBS — Post Traumatic Ballard Syndrome. We must be there for one another. We must be strong. We must move on.

GAME DAY AFFIRMATION

I will try to forgive Harold Ballard — not to excuse his behaviour, but to allow me to move on with my life and allow the healing to begin.

GAME 59

> *How would you like a job where, every time you make a mistake, a big red light goes on and 18,000 people boo?*
>
> — Jacques Plante, Montreal Canadiens great, Hall of Fame goalie, and former (although nobody remembers) Leaf star

There are a lot of unsung heroes in Leafs Nation, but one of the most unjustly overlooked alumni is Jacques Plante.

Of course, fans know his name. A seven-time All-Star and Vezina Trophy winner with six Stanley Cup rings, Plante was the mainstay of the Montreal Canadiens during their dynastic six-Cup decade, 1953–1963. But Leafs Nation forgets that he played 106 games for Toronto, including an overlooked season for the ages.

Plante came to town in 1970, 42 years old, three years out of a too-early retirement. He played 40 games for Toronto that year, registering 24 wins and four shutouts — almost single-handedly lifting the Leafs to a respectable fourth-place finish. Most impressive: his 1.88 goals against average, which was best in the league (compared to the other Leafs keepers who, combined, had a dismal 3.39 goals against average).

But there's more. Plante played before the NHL kept track of save percentages — saves divided by shots — which is considered the best measure of a goalie's performance. Number crunchers have looked at the 1971 season retroactively and discovered that Plante finished the year with a .942 save percentage. Not only was it the highest of his career and the highest of any goalie in the league that season, it was the highest save percentage in NHL history ... proving that you can teach an old dog new tricks, and even Leafs players can succeed every once in a while.

GAME DAY AFFIRMATION

Today I will reflect on the lesson of Jacques Plante — that the greatest achievements often go unnoticed — and recognize that, even in the aftermath of a truly crappy season, a good statistician can always help us find a reason to be optimistic.

GAME 60

> *Love and compassion are necessities, not luxuries.*
> *Without them humanity cannot survive.*

— Dalai Lama, religious figure and everyone's favourite Lama

Think about the worst thing that's happened to the Leafs. The game that left you with the most stomach-churning, mind-numbing, soul-shattering feeling of hatred and despair. Reach deep into the chasms of your mind and remember that feeling ...

Deeper ...

Deeper ...

Keep going ...

Okay, stop! You don't want to go too far down.

Did you retrieve the feeling? Was it after the 14–4 loss to Buffalo in 1981 (the biggest margin of defeat in Leafs history)? Was it after game 11 of our 11-game losing streak of 2015 (longest losing streak in Leafs history)? Was it the 1981–1982 or 1985–1986 season, when the Leafs finished with 20 wins, the lowest in the NHL's modern era? Was it the crushing, go-from-ahead collapse in the final 11 minutes of Game 7 of the first round playoff loss to the Boston Bruins in 2013?

These moments could cause anyone to think some pretty negative things, to despise their team or their favourite players. Even worse, they may cause you — a recovering Leafs fan — to be critical of yourself.

It's at these dark moments of the soul that we need to strive for a little something called compassion. Compassion — our ability to sympathize with other humans, empathize, feel their pain, understand their situation — is the cornerstone of emotional health. When we respond to the misery of others with kindness and acceptance, we are opening our minds to treating ourselves with compassion. No matter how great the goal differential, how long the losing streak, how short-sighted and pinheaded the trade, we must respond with mindful compassion and, in the process, move ourselves one step closer to peace.

Or peas, if we're feeling peckish and want a healthy snack.

GAME DAY AFFIRMATION

Today I will practise compassion, responding with kindness and understanding every time the ref or linesman makes a stupid call or misses an obvious offside, the defender fails to clear the puck on the penalty kill, and that forward makes one too many moves and fails to get a shot on net. Crap: it's going to be a long game.

GAME 61

Monsters cannot be announced. One cannot say: "Here are our monsters," without immediately turning the monsters into pets.

— Jacques Derrida, philosopher and guy who knows an unusual amount about monsters

Harold Ballard's on-ice record was bad (during his 19-year tenure as Leafs boss, the team had only six winning seasons, and missed the playoffs as often as not) but not as bad as his off-ice record (49 charges, three convictions, and hard time in the Kingston Penitentiary, Millhaven, and a Toronto halfway house).

It all started — legally speaking — back in 1968, when the RCMP raided the offices of Maple Leaf Gardens and left with several boxes of documents. Several months later, the shoe finally dropped. The cops charged Ballard and Stafford Smythe with 49 counts each — for offences that included fraud, theft, and tax evasion. Among other things, Ballard was accused of diverting $200,000 — $1.5 million in today's dollars — to renovate his house and cottage, rent limos for his daughter's wedding, buy motorcycles for his sons — and pad a joint bank account he shared with Stafford Smythe.

Ballard pleaded not guilty, but the judge found him guilty on all but two counts and sentenced him to nine years in prison. After a short stay at the hardcore Kingston Penitentiary, Ballard was transferred to Millhaven minimum-security prison in Bath, Ontario.

Ballard would later brag that his stint in Millhaven was like being in a country club: he drank beer with the guards, enjoyed steak dinners, and watched whatever he liked on his own colour TV.

In October 1973, Ballard was released on parole and found himself with a stranglehold on the Leafs' budding empire. His old crony, Stafford Smythe, had died in 1971, waiting for his own trial to come up, and Ballard had bought up all of Smythe's Leafs shares. He now had a 60 percent stake in the team. Ballard made short work of the Leafs board, squeezing out all opposition at the ownership level and setting to work, in earnest, to make life miserable for the Leafs and their fans ... for generations to come.

GAME DAY AFFIRMATION

Today I will recognize the pain Harold Ballard has caused in my life, embrace my PTBS mindfully, and look forward to the comfort and relief a healthy Shanaplan will bring me.

GAME 62

> *Life has meaning only in the struggle. Triumph or defeat is in the hands of the Gods. So let us celebrate the struggle.*
>
> — Stevie Wonder, singer, songwriter, music producer, and probably coolest guy ever (next to Conn Smythe)

Conn Smythe was a hockey god.

But even gods — as we learned in *Star Trek V: The Voyage Home* — can grow weary. And by 1962, the Major found the day-to-day business of running a hockey empire to be more than a minor headache.

In 1962, on the heels of the Leafs 10th Stanley Cup with Smythe at the helm, the Major sold 45,000 of his 50,000 shares in Maple Leaf Gardens Ltd. to a consortium that included his son Stafford, Stafford's crony Harold Ballard, and newspaper mogul John Bassett. Conn Smythe pocketed $2.3 million in the deal — that's more than $18 million in today's dollars — and turned the chairmanship of the board of directors over to his son.

Smythe focused most of his efforts on his stable of champion thoroughbreds, although he still kept his hands — and his nose — in the game he loved. He publicly fought with Canadian prime minister Lester B. Pearson for wanting to replace the old flag — the Red Ensign — with the new-fangled Maple Leaf (you'd think he would have appreciated the publicity), and tried, unsuccessfully, to block the new flag from flying at Maple Leaf Gardens.

And don't get him started about expansion. Smythe was vehemently opposed to doubling the size of the league, saying that adding six teams would water down the game (although, to be fair, when Smythe started in the NHL it was a 10-team league).

The Major suffered a heart attack in 1978. A fighter to the end, he hung in for another two years, but he finally passed away on November 18, 1980, leaving behind a legacy of 13 Stanley Cup wins and a hockey dynasty that would fuel the hearts and minds of recovering Leafs fans past, present, and future.

GAME DAY AFFIRMATION

Today I will remember the life and legacy of Conn Smythe, and remind myself how much we can achieve if we only set our minds to it.

GAME 63

> *By believing passionately in something that still does not exist, we create it. The non-existent is whatever we have not sufficiently desired.*
>
> — Franz Kafka, writer and sharer of first name with Franz Ferdinand

Harold Ballard laid many of the tracks that would become the train wreck known as the Toronto Maple Leafs ... and one of these tracks was underestimating the World Hockey Association.

The WHA began in 1972, just as Ballard was enjoying the country club lifestyle of Millhaven prison. The new league had a simple business plan: expand the sport (by putting teams in the major NHL-less U.S. markets and secondary Canadian cities that could sustain a team) and stealing stars from the NHL by paying marquee players fairly.

The plan worked — sort of. The league launched in 1972 with 12 teams: the Alberta Oilers, Chicago Cougars, Cleveland Crusaders, Houston Aeros, L.A. Sharks, Minnesota Fighting Saints, New England Whalers, New

York Raiders, Ottawa Nationals, Philadelphia Blazers, Quebec Nordiques, and Winnipeg Jets.

The new league also managed to convince 67 NHLers to make the jump. And it wasn't just a bunch of nobodies: there were legitimate stars like Derek Sanderson, J.C. Tremblay, Bernie Parent, and Gerry Cheevers, along with the biggest prize of all, Bobby Hull, who signed with the Winnipeg Jets for a record 10-year, $2.7-million contract (that's more than $16 million in today's dollars, folks).

At the start, the Leafs weren't too badly impacted by the WHA. They lost a couple of young defenders — Rick Ley and Brad Selwood — and veteran forward Jim Harrison, but that was it. For his part, Ballard didn't put much stock in the new league and fully expected them to fold before the year ended.

While the WHA experienced a lot of growing pains in its first year of operation, it did make it to year two — and had a surprise in store for Ballard in the form of the new Toronto Toros franchise.

Never one to turn down a dollar, Ballard let the upstart Toros rent Maple Leaf Gardens, although not without the usual Ballardian antics. He dimmed the Gardens' lights during the Toros' home opener, and demanded that team owners pay extra to have the lights turned up. He also took away the cushions on the home bench's seats, figuring, maybe, that it would be harder for the Toros' players to skate with sore bums.

In the end, though, the WHA cost Ballard more than an inconvenient tenant. He lost budding superstar goalie Bernie Parent to the new league, and a year later, Leafs Nation was shocked when Dave Keon — the captain and face of the franchise — bolted to go play for the WHA's Minnesota Fighting Saints. It didn't just signal the end of a Keon era in Toronto, it also heralded a new economic reality — one that completely went over Ballard's head. The NHL was no longer a monopoly. Players now had options. The days of owners ruling with an iron fist — and cheapskating their skaters — was over.

It was a new reality Ballard refused to accept. And it would cost his team and its fans dearly in the years to come.

GAME DAY AFFIRMATION

Today I will remember those (mostly) long-forgotten teams from the WHA's first season, and remind myself that like these teams, I am but a pebble dropped in the ocean. Who knows what will come from the ripples I cause?

GAME 64

Don't cry because it's over. Smile because it happened.

— Theodor Seuss Geisel, semi-licensed physician

Great players make great teams. Building a team with talented individuals is a simple, time-tested strategy that creates success in just about every professional sport. And the history of our Leafs is brimming with the inclusion of great players, but seemingly as equally littered with great players leaving. Whether for greener pastures, thicker wallets, or calmer heads, or by the clumsy/fiery hands of management, many skilled players have left Toronto to play elsewhere.

Think you know your Leafs trivia? Try matching the player with the circumstances surrounding his departure from the Leafs.

1. Bernie Parent — A. The Leafs traded his hefty contract away to New Jersey in a cost-cutting measure. He didn't complain.

2. Doug Gilmour — B. Signed with the Florida Panthers as an unrestricted free agent after Toronto offered him less money than he was worth.

3. Curtis Joseph — C. Left to sign with the World Hockey Association — his wife wasn't exactly captivated by Toronto's city whimsy. Nothing personal.

4. Darryl Sittler — D. Traded to the Philadelphia Flyers, his relationship with the organization at an all-time low.

5. Mats Sundin — E. Butted heads with Harold Ballard; bailed to WHA when Ballard wouldn't trade him.

6. Gary Roberts — F. A fan favourite, traded away to the Quebec Nordiques.

7. Wendel Clark — G. Apparently wasn't the biggest lover of Pat Quinn's coaching style — headed to the Detroit Red Wings with a sour taste in his mouth.

8. Dave Keon — H. Stalemated the organization by neither renegotiating his contract with them nor waiving his no-trade clause. Eventually signed with the Vancouver Canucks. Not cool, dude. Not cool.

Answers

1—C   2—A   3—G   4—D
5—H   6—B   7—F   8—E

GAME DAY AFFIRMATION

Today I will accept things as they come. I won't dwell on what might have been or what could be. I will focus on what is. Unless it's another blowout; in that case, I'll just change the channel.

GAME 65

*Darkness cannot drive out darkness: only light can do that.
Hate cannot drive out hate: only love can do that.*

— Dr. Martin Luther King Jr., the original Doc Martin

The Toronto Maple Leafs have a history of soft-spoken, hard-working gentlemen who proudly wore the "C" and led the team by effort and example. Add to that list a certain Darryl Sittler, the quintessential Leafs gentleman hero, blessed with as soft a pair of hands as the game has ever seen.

Sittler came to the Leafs from the London Knights, an Ontario Hockey League Junior A team where he had developed under the watchful eye of another Leafs legend, Knights' coach Turk Broda. Come the 1970 NHL draft, Toronto picked Sittler eighth overall — sandwiched between a pair of RPs (just after Rob Polis, right before Ron Plumb).

Sittler got off to a slow start with the Leafs. In 1970–1971, he saw limited action and finished with just 49 games and 18 points. Season two saw Sittler get in 74 games and up his scoring to 15 goals and 32 total points. But by season three, Sittler had caught fire: 29 goals, 48 assists, for a team-leading 77 points.

Throughout his tenure as captain, Sittler embraced his leadership role, galvanized his teams, and let his hard work speak for itself. Two years later, when a disgruntled Dave Keon bolted for the WHA's greener pastures, Sittler was made Leafs captain. He responded with his best season to date: 41 goals, 59 assists, to become the Leafs' first ever 100-point man.

Sittler played the better part of 12 seasons with the Buds (the less said about his departure, the better), and ended his NHL career with 1,096 games (844 as a Leaf), 484 goals (his 389 goals as a Leaf are second only to Mats Sundin), 637 assists (527 as a Leaf, third best in team history), and 1,121 points (916 as a Leaf, second only to, once again, Sundin).

Sittler remains one of Toronto's finest ambassadors. And, as a constant reminder, we are left with his famous Number 27 hanging from the Air Canada Centre rafters, a beacon of light for recovering Leafs fans everywhere, reminding us that no matter what happens on the ice, there is a still a great tradition behind us, guiding us, hopefully, through the storm.

GAME DAY AFFIRMATION

Today I will look to the rafters of my house and find my own personal beacon — a fly, perhaps, or a chip in the paint — to guide me through my darkest storms. And I will call this beacon Darryl.

GAME 66

> *Let it go.*
>
> — Elsa, Queen of Arendelle and budding Buddhist philosopher

Non-attachment. It sounds a little bit like an oxymoron, like Jumbo Shrimp, Fun Run, or CBC Entertainment.

But as you strive toward mindfulness, non-attachment is a critical component. It's called enlightenment for a reason: not only are you illuminating your path, you are lightening your load.

Non-attachment is a simple concept to grasp. Think about your favourite Leafs sweater — the one your girlfriend made you give to Goodwill because you'd had it for like 15 years and it was too small and full of holes, and while it didn't completely smell like ass, it was definitely heading in that direction …

You know the sweater I'm talking about.

Non-attachment is the process of giving things away — our real and metaphorical and/or emotional Leafs jerseys — letting go, saying goodbye, and moving on.

The 1993–1994 Leafs provide an illustrative example.

The Harold Ballard days were gone (they were pretty easy to be non-attached to, frankly) and the Leafs were coming off a stellar 43–29–12 campaign that saw them go all the way to the Western Conference Finals (losing in five to those damn Vancouver Canucks).

Cliff Fletcher was general manager and at the top of his game.

He had a tough choice to make. Two years earlier, he had made a major swap with the Edmonton Oilers, sending them five players (including the team's top offensive threat Vince Damphousse, defensive stalwart Luke Richardson, and a tough youngster named Scott Thornton) for Craig Berube and a couple of future Hall of Famers in Glenn Anderson and goaltending superstar Grant Fuhr.

Fletcher's dilemma? He had a hot young sophomore goalie in Felix Potvin, making Fuhr an expensive but valuable option. The fact was, the Leafs really needed help up front, not on the back end. Fletcher knew he had to do something and that, in order to get something of value, he would have to give up something of value in return. So he swung a deal with the Buffalo Sabres, trading away Fuhr and a fifth-round draft pick for offensive sparkplug Dave Andreychuk and a first-rounder.

Not done with non-attachment ways, Fletcher made an even bigger deal during the NHL draft that June, sending Leafs left-winger Wendel Clark (along with defenceman

Sylvain Lefebvre, 19-year-old prospect Landon Wilson, and the 22nd overall pick to the Quebec Nordiques for a guy named Mats Sundin (with defencemen Garth Butcher, forward Todd Warriner, and the 10th pick in the draft).

It was a gutsy move, trading Toronto's most popular player — coming off a career-best 46-goal, 76-point performance — for a budding young superstar in the midst of a contract dispute.

In both cases, Fletcher orchestrated a kind of lose–lose, win–win. Each team had to give up something cherished; in return, both acquired something they really needed. And that's what non-attachment is all about — letting go of something valuable to get something valuable in return.

GAME DAY AFFIRMATION

Today I will let go of something important to me (even if it's just that jalapeno Pringle you and your buddy both accidently grabbed at the same time).

GAME 67

> *The most painful state of being is remembering the future, particularly the one you'll never have.*
>
> — Søren Kierkegaard, philosopher and forward thinker

Stonehenge. Atlantis. The Giant Heads of Easter Island. Donald Trump's hair. Do curious objects and structures hold powerful mysteries, the truth of which we have yet to uncover? Are there mysterious forces at work, beyond human comprehension?

And what of the most mysterious structures of all: the pyramids of Egypt? What power do they hold?

Probably not much. But back in the 1970s, pyramid power was all the rage. There was something to the shape of the thing that created a kind of magnetic energy field or something. No one was really sure what. Still, you could, it was claimed, preserve food and sharpen razors merely by placing the items inside a pyramid, and sleeping with a pyramid under your bed could improve your health, emotional outlook, and even sexual performance.

A strategically placed pyramid could even help you win a hockey game. At least that's what Leafs coach Red Kelly told his team. It was April 22, 1976, and the team was in the midst of a dramatic playoff run against the hated — and Stanley Cup–defending — Philadelphia Flyers.

The Flyers made a big thing about their own mysterious force, trotting out good luck charm Kate Smith to sing "God Bless America" at the start of every home game. Kelly knew he needed a distraction of his own to get his players' minds off the Flyers' voodoo.

He wasn't sure what to do, but then Kelly had a great idea. His daughter had "cured" her migraine by placing a pyramid under her bed while she slept. What if he put a few pyramids under the Leafs' bench during the game.

The result? Leafs start centre Darryl Sittler exploded for a record-tying five goals and the Leafs won the game 8–5, sending the series to Game 6.

The Leafs' pyramid mojo was short-lived, however, and they lost the next game 7–3 and were eliminated from the playoffs. But the memory of pyramid power lives on the minds of recovering Leafs fans to this day....

GAME DAY AFFIRMATION

Today I will honour the memory of two Leafs greats — Red Kelly and Darryl Sittler — by making a small pyramid out of popsicle sticks and putting it under my sofa while I watch the game. What can I say? I'm easily amused.

GAME 68

Mistakes are proof you are trying.

— Unknown, a famous quotemaster
and close cousin to Anonymous

It wasn't exactly of Biblical proportions, but it was a Second Coming.

It was 1979, and the Leafs had just finished a strong season — a semifinal loss to the powerhouse Montreal Canadiens was nothing to sneeze at — and were widely regarded as a young team full of promise.

In the midst of that, Ballard decided that a change of GMs was in store. He fired long-time honcho Jim Gregory — whose teams had made the playoffs in eight of ten years — and replaced him with the man he had replaced, a blustery blast from the past named Punch Imlach.

Imlach had just come off an eight-year stint with the Buffalo Sabres, shaping them into one of the NHL's most successful expansion teams ever. Imlach had built a strong team around stars Gilbert Perreault and Rick Martin. As time passed, however, the lustre wore off, and as the famous Imlach magic touch had faded, the infamous Imlach heavy hand had become more pronounced. After too many player feuds and on-ice losses, the Sabres showed Imlach the door.

The return to the Leafs didn't help. Always a little off the wall, Imlach drifted further and further away from reality with every passing day. His old-school disciplinarian tactics no longer worked on the generation of post-WHA players. When he told them to wear suits and ties to the Leafs office, the players laughed behind his back and openly defied him. Tiger Williams was fined twice for not donning a necktie before Imlach gave up.

More seriously, he feuded with the team's undisputed leader and superstar, Darryl Sittler. He disliked Sittler's influence in the dressing room, and wasn't a fan of the upstart players' union, which Sittler strongly supported.

Things came to a head when Imlach tried to take his own players to court to prevent them from taking part in *Hockey Night in Canada*'s intermission "Showdown Shootout" series. Imlach's effort to get a court order went nowhere, but the battle lines were drawn.

Imlach couldn't get at Sittler directly because the captain had a no-trade clause in his contract. Instead, he went after Sittler's best friend and teammate, Lanny McDonald.

McDonald was an undisputed star and scoring stud, coming off three straight 40-plus goal seasons. Not to mention

McDonald's playoff heroics the previous spring. In the quarter-final Stanley Cup series against the highly favoured New York Islanders, McDonald scored the Game 7 overtime series-winning goal … with a broken nose and wrist.

But in Imlach's mind, being Sittler's friend was bad news for McDonald. And being the Leafs National Hockey League Players' Association representative only made things worse.

On December 28, 1979, Imlach pulled the trigger on a deal that shocked, if not the hockey world, at least his team's coach, Floyd Smith. Imlach sent McDonald — in the prime of his career — and defenceman Joel Quenneville to Colorado in return for veteran wings Wilf Paiement and Pat Hickey.

McDonald went on to have a long and productive career — including a 66-goal campaign with the Calgary Flames in 1982–1983, and a Stanley Cup in 1988–1989. Imlach went on to more infamy and is remembered to this day as both the best *and* worst general manager Leafs fans have ever seen.

GAME DAY AFFIRMATION

Today I will strive to rise above the petty distractions of the day and focus, like the glory-days-era Imlach, on the power of positive thinking, and not, like the small-minded-start-the-Leafs-onto-the-road-to-futility-era Imlach, on the little things that never really add up to a hill of beans.

GAME 69

> *Grief can be the garden of compassion. If you keep your heart open through everything, your pain can become your greatest ally in your life's search for love and wisdom.*

— Rumi, Persian poet, philosopher, and mystical overachiever

On January 20, 1982, Toronto Maple Leafs fans woke up to the shocking reality: Darryl Sittler, the team's 31-year-old superstar captain, had been traded to the hated Philadelphia Flyers.

In return, the Leafs got Rich Costello (who went on to a 12-game, four-point NHL career), a second-round pick in the 1982 draft (which turned out to be a pretty good Peter Ihnačák), and Ken "Player to Be Named Later" Strong (15 NHL games, four points).

Leafs fans didn't know what to think: it was as if their very hearts had been torn from their chests.

What they were experiencing is common to Toronto's hockey faithful, a mental process we can call the five stages of post-Leafs-trade grief (PLTG). This is based on the pioneering work of Swiss psychiatrist Elisabeth Kübler-Ross, who first wrote about the five stages of grief in her 1969 bestseller *On Death and Dying*. While she may not have specifically had Leafs trades in mind, her work has proved surprisingly prescient. The stages of PLTG include:

1. Denial. How do we react when we find out our favourite player has been traded? Initially, we are in a state of shock, and often try to deny the swap has taken place. *Carlo Colaiacovo and Alex Steen for Lee Stempniak?* we say. *Preposterous! Sports Centre must have made a mistake! No GM in his right mind would do such a thing!* It's a natural reaction, as our mind and hearts need time to adjust to the shocking loss.
2. Anger. When the reality of the situation finally sinks in, we often respond with anger and resentment. *What kind of idiot would make a trade like that,* we say. *That's it; I'm done with this goddamned team and its goddamned stupid trades!* Again, it's a way of distancing ourselves from the painful truth and using anger as a bridge that drives us away from the source of our pain — the Leafs — while keeping the relationship (anger does require engagement, after all) alive.
3. Bargaining. Once we get over the anger, we begin to actually process what happened. We are unconsciously aware that we are in a tough situation — we love the Leafs, but how can we love the Leafs when they've hurt

us *and* traded away our favourite player? The answer: we make a mental bargain. We promise to be better people, better Leafs fans, if only the draft pick or player to be named turns out to be a superstar. It's a desperate act, but these are desperate times.

4. Depression. Eventually, the reality of the situation sinks in. Sittler is gone, off to Philadelphia, to wear those stupid Cooperalls, score 83 points, and get named to the NHL All-Star team; we are stuck with a guy named Costello who can barely crack the Leafs' diminished lineup. Life in Leafs Nation has never been so terrible. With so much relentless misery, why even *be* a Leafs fan at all? Actually, it's hard to argue with that. It's during this stage of PLTG that we often grow sullen and irritable, eat at Hooters a lot, wear track pants in public, and indulge in other anti-social and self-defeating behaviours. That is, until we reach the stage of ...

5. Acceptance. Sometimes, you just have to give in and accept the cards that fate — and the Maple Leafs — have dealt you. This is the point of acceptance, that mindful, philosophical position where you are able to look at the trade with clear eyes, understand that it was nothing personal and that you were only a patient observer to its unfolding. Being angry at the trade is pointless: it's like being angry at one of

Don Cherry's rambling things-were-better-in-my-day Coach's Corner tirades. Sittler is gone. There is nothing you can do (other than, heaven forbid, stop loving the Leafs). It's time to accept the way things are and move on ...

GAME DAY AFFIRMATION

Today I will accept that trades are a part of life in the NHL ... just as I will accept that ongoing grief is part of my process as a recovering Leafs fan.

GAME 70

I guess one of the ways that karma works is that it finds out what you are most afraid of and then makes that happen eventually.

— Cheech Marin, stoner comedian and Chong's better half

Three times isn't always a charm. Just ask Wendel Clark: Captain Crunch served three separate tours of duty with the Leafs, and while the last one was short, it wasn't particularly sweet.

Clark's first stint with the Leafs started in 1985, when the Buds selected him first overall in the draft. He was a highly touted Saskatchewan farm boy who'd been a standout on Canada's gold medal–winning team at the World Junior Championships and had put up 87 points with the Western Hockey League's Saskatoon Blades ... all as a *defender*.

But Clark never played a shift on defence with the Leafs. With shades of Red Kelly, the Leafs' second-year coach Dan Maloney switched Clark to left wing ... and the magic happened. Clark finished the year with 34 goals and 45 points — good for a selection to the NHL All-Rookie Team —

while proving that he wasn't just another pretty face. He wasn't afraid to drop the gloves with anyone, and by the end of the year, he had accumulated 227 penalty minutes (although, that total paled in comparison to the 377 minutes racked up by Clark's cousin, Detroit Red Wings enforcer Joey Kocur).

Clark's first stint with the Leafs lasted nine seasons, four of those as captain, and over that period he played 530 playoff and regular season games, scoring 239 goals and racking up 509 total points.

At the end of the 1993–1994 season, the Leafs dealt Clark to the Quebec Nordiques in a multi-player deal that landed Mats Sundin in Toronto. Clark went on to an injury-filled, so-so season in la belle province, and when the Nordiques moved to Colorado the following season, the team dealt him to the Islanders. But he was soon back in the Leafs' lineup in a trade deadline deal. Clark played another two full seasons with the Leafs after that, adding 125 games to his Toronto totals, along with 50 goals and 83 points.

The Leafs didn't re-sign him at the end of the 1997–1998 season, though, and Clark joined the Tampa Bay Lightning as a free agent. He had a huge comeback season in the Florida sunshine: 28 goals, 42 points, and a place on the North American team at the All-Star game, before being traded to the Detroit Red Wings in another late-season deal.

Clark was really only a rental in Motown, and the next season he signed with the Chicago Blackhawks. But age and the ravages of playing tough every night had taken their toll. Clark struggled with back problems the entire time with the team, limiting his play to 13 games. The Blackhawks left Clark unprotected on the waiver wire, and the Leafs rookie general manager Pat Quinn picked him up for one more kick at the can.

It almost worked ... sort of. While Clark didn't fare well in his final 20 regular season games — scoring just two goals and notching two assists — his return gave the team an emotional burst. The Leafs were already playing great and were on their way to the first 100-point season in franchise history.

Quinn banked on Clark being an inspirational presence in the dressing room as the team prepared for the playoffs. The GM was right, but it wasn't enough to get the Leafs past Martin Brodeur and the (eventual Stanley Cup–winning) New Jersey Devils.

And thus, Clark's third time round in Toronto ended — as did his career — with neither a bang nor a whimper, just a happy homecoming, with one Leafs legend back where he belonged.

GAME DAY AFFIRMATION

Today I will pay attention to my home and take stock of the things I love and cherish. I will also beat the crap out of Marty McSorley if he cheap-shots any of my players.

GAME 71

> *Let the one among you who is without sin be the first to cast a stone.*
>
> — Jesus Christ, unwitting religious leader and all-around good guy

Judgments.

We all make them — about places, players, the quality of arena snacks, Montreal fans ...

Whether good or bad, we are conditioned to judge based on our own experiences. The problem is, being judgmental makes it hard to be mindful. Judging the imperfection of people and things keeps us focused on the negative, and also sets a pattern for our own internal voice. When we judge harshly, we also tend to judge ourselves the same way.

As recovering Leafs fans, striving to reach a place of non-judgment, we can learn a lesson from one of Toronto's greatest enforcers, David "Tiger" Williams.

Tiger was a brutal force of nature who played like a predator on the ice, always looking for his next victim. Standing just 5 feet 7 inches and weighing 190 pounds, Williams was never the biggest man on the ice (and never a stranger to the penalty box: his 3,966 minutes in the sin bin is still an NHL record). But his opponents feared him. And not just because he finished his career with 246 fights. They knew that Tiger didn't discriminate: big or small, nice or nasty, if you asked for it, Tiger would punch you in the face no matter what.

You see, Tiger was never preoccupied by whether or not an experience would be good or bad; he would simply observe his thoughts and let them be.

Well, maybe he wasn't like that, but his actions certainly seemed that way. And who are we to judge, right?

GAME DAY AFFIRMATION

Today I will face everything with ferocious non-judgment, just like Tiger would.

GAME 72

> *Skåda inte given häst i mun.*
>
> — Old Swedish saying (told to us by an old Swede)

Sundin and Salming — how Swede they are.

Together, the pair hold at least 17 season and/or career Leafs records. Who's the best? It's impossible to say. All we know is that the history of the Leafs would not be the same if it weren't for this pair of Swedish meatballs.

First, Börje Salming, one of the greatest Leafs — and greatest NHL — blueliners ever. Signed as an undrafted player in 1973 (and without the knowledge of Harold Ballard, who was locked up in the Millhaven country club at the time) by Leafs scout Gerry McNamara, Salming came to Toronto a virtual nobody.

But he quickly put the NHL on notice, notching 39 points in his rookie season and impressing everyone with his speed, skill, and toughness.

By the time he finished with the Leafs in 1989, he had racked up the third highest number of games (1,099; behind George Armstrong and Tim Horton) and a slew of records, including: most assists in team history (620), most total points by a Leafs defenceman (768), most assists in one season by a Leafs defenceman (66), and the best career plus/minus (+155) — not to mention the NHL record for most career points by an undrafted defenceman (787).

And then there's Mats Sundin. Arguably the greatest Leafs player of all time, Sundin retired from the game as the team's all-time leader in goals (420) and points (987), and second only to Salming himself in both assists (567) and plus/minus (+99).

Throughout his career — which included stops with the Quebec Nordiques and the Vancouver Canucks — Sundin maintained a better than point-a-game pace (1,349 points in 1,346 games), played in every All-Star game between 1996 and 2004 (except for 2003, due to injuries), and became only the second Swedish-born player — after, you guessed it, Salming — to be inducted into the NHL Hall of Fame.

GAME DAY AFFIRMATION

Today I will accept every person on their own merits, without comparing them. I will also eat some Swedish meatballs. They sound tasty.

GAME 73

Our dead are never dead to us, until we have forgotten them.

— George Eliot, chick writer with dude name

Harold Ballard died on April 11, 1990. Not surprisingly, it wasn't a quiet passing.

For one thing, there was the little problem of Yolanda Ballard. She was Harold's long-time companion, who legally changed her name to Ballard though the two never actually married. Yolanda, it seemed, didn't get along well with Ballard's children, Bill, Harold Jr., and Mary Elizabeth.

How not well? you may ask.

Well, the previous year, Bill was arrested for assaulting Yolanda. Seems she was escorting him out of Ballard's Maple Leaf Gardens apartment — showing him the door as it were — and he responded by punching her in the face and kicking her in the stomach. A judge ultimately found Bill Ballard guilty and ordered him to pay a $500 fine ... which pales in comparison to the $15 million (almost $29 million in today's dollars) he got when he sold the share of Maple Leafs stock his dad had given him.

In the aftermath of Harold Ballard's death, Yolanda sued the estate. Harold had bequeathed her a $50,000 annual stipend, but she felt she deserved more. She put in a bid for $381,000 a year; the courts finally settled at just over $90,000.

The courtroom antics almost overshadowed Ballard's death ... and for many Leafs fans it took a while to realize that the Ballard era had come to an end.

It was replaced by a new era of relative instability. There were a series of ownership shifts that it would take a forensic accountant to understand, but none of it seemed to make a difference on the ice. In fact, the Leafs have only made the playoffs five times in the last 15 Ballardless years; in the previous Ballardful years, they made the playoffs 10 times.

Maybe Ballard wasn't the problem. Maybe there's something in the Lake Ontario water that makes the Leafs do so poorly.

In any case, rest in peace, Harold Ballard. The time has come to move on ...

GAME DAY AFFIRMATION

Today I will accept, once and for all, that Harold Ballard is dead and gone, and that he really can't be blamed for what's happened to the Leafs since then. Besides, Harold didn't force me to be a Leafs fan ... and isn't preventing me from moving forward in my recovery.

GAME 74

> *May you have the hindsight to know where you've been,*
> *the foresight to know where you are going, and the*
> *insight to know when you have gone too far.*
>
> — Mike, an old Irish guy we ran into at a bar once

From the Toronto St. Pats to Brendan Shanahan — and all the King Clancys, Red Kellys, Pat Burnses, and Brian Burkes in between — the Leafs have had a long-standing love affair with things Irish. And that love reached new highs in the late 1990s with the arrival of a new head coach, a feisty, elegant Irishman named Pat Quinn.

It was actually Quinn's second go-round with the Leafs. Twenty years earlier, he had patrolled the Leafs' blue line, accumulating 99 games and 183 penalty minutes in his two seasons with the Buds (and entering hockey lore by catching Bobby Orr in his own end with his head down and knocking the Bruins superstar out cold with an elbow).

Quinn went on to play nine seasons in the NHL, gaining a reputation as a tough, defence-first defender who didn't mind dropping the gloves when he had to.

Quinn's transition from player to coach was seamless. After a few seasons in the Philadelphia Flyers organization, he was finally made head coach 50 games into the 1978–1979 season. The team did well, posting 18 wins in their final 30 games.

The following year, Quinn took his Flyers on a record-breaking tear. The team didn't lose a single game from October 14 to January 6 — 35 straight games (25 wins, 10 ties) without a loss. The Flyers carried the momentum into the playoffs, making it all the way to the Stanley Cup Finals (although they ultimately bowed out to the New York Islanders in six games).

Then followed stints with Los Angeles (where he increased the team total by 23 points over the previous season) and Vancouver (where he added general manager and team president to his resumé, as well as another Jack Adams Award for coach of the year, and even earned another trip to the Stanley Cup Finals).

The Leafs turned to Quinn in the aftermath of the 1997–1998 season, when the team finished 10th in the Western Conference and out of the playoff picture.

Under Quinn, the transformation was incredible. The Leafs went from a plodding defensive workhorse to a freewheeling, high-speed thoroughbred in the blink of an eye, racking up 97 points that season and a fourth-place Eastern Conference finish.

And the team kept flying, all the way to the conference finals (where they lost in five games to the Buffalo Sabres). It was the Leafs' best run since the 1993–1994 season, when they'd lost in a semifinal round to the Quinn-coached Vancouver Canucks.

The playoff success was a harbinger of things to come. The Leafs made the post-season the next six years in row, advancing to the conference finals one more time and the conference semifinals three times.

Quinn's days in Toronto came to an end after the 2005–2006 season. The Leafs had finished fourth in the Northeast Division and failed to make the playoffs. Amid backroom turmoil — which included the arrival of John Ferguson Jr., who replaced Quinn as Leafs GM — and an uncertain ownership future, Quinn was let go.

He left town with his head held high: 300 wins, second only to Punch Imlach, and a .501 winning percentage, the highest of any coach in Leafs history.

GAME DAY AFFIRMATION

Today, regardless of whether the Leafs win or lose, I will dance a little jig in Pat Quinn's memory.

GAME 75

> *Don't blame the boss. He has enough problems.*
>
> — Donald Rumsfeld, U.S. secretary of defense and Golden Raspberry Worst Supporting Actor award recipient

September 3, 1981: Punch Imlach suffers his third heart attack. Although never officially fired as coach, he would never work for the Leafs organization again. He left a spotty legacy, but facts cannot be disputed: 760 games; 365 wins. Both team records.

Flash forward to May 15, 2015: Leafs president Brendan "Shanaplan" Shanahan announces that the team has a new coach: Mike Babcock.

The Leafs stole Babcock at the 11th hour from underneath the Buffalo Sabres' collective noses on the strength of an eight-year, $50 million deal (making him the highest-paid coach in hockey history, although his yearly stipend pales in comparison to the $24 million Brazil's Luiz Felipe Scolari got for coaching Uzbekistan FC Bunyodkor for the 2009 season).

Babcock was introduced to fans and media as the Leafs' 30th head coach (39th if you count the ones from the Arenas and St. Pats).

What of the other coaches that came before Babcock? Put your Leafs trivia knowledge to the test with this little head coach quiz.

1. The Leafs have had a lot of head coaches, but only a handful have won Stanley Cups. How many have won, and can you name them?
2. Who of the following was not a Leafs coach: Art Duncan, Billy Reay, John McLellan, Joe Crozier, or Nick Beverley?
3. One person coached the Leafs three separate times. Who?
4. Which coach* has the worst winning percentage in Leafs history?
5. Which coach was behind the bench for the fewest number of games?
6. Hap Day, Joe Primeau, King Clancy, Dick Duff, Howie Meeker, and George Armstrong were all well-known Leafs players who went on to coach the team. Which of the following coaches was also a former Leafs player: Mike Nykoluk, Joe Crozier, Dan Maloney, George Armstrong, Randy Carlyle, or Ron Wilson?
7. Who's missing from the above list?
8. Two coaches hired themselves, but only one fired himself. Who were they?

Answers

1. Four: Dick Irvin (1932), Hap Day (1942, 1945, 1947–1949), Busher Jackson (1951), and Punch Imlach (1962–1964, 1967).
2. Trick question: they were all Leafs coaches: Duncan (1930–1931), Reay (1957–1958), McLelland (1969–1973), Crozier (1980–1981), and Beverley (1996).
3. King Clancy, who served as head coach for 210 games from 1953–1956, and as interim coach in 1966 and again, for two games, in 1990.
4. Dan Maloney, who coached 160 games from 1984–1986, had a .328 winning percentage. The asterisk belongs to Peter Horachek, who served as sacrificial lamb ... we mean interim coach ... for 40 games in 2015, putting together a truly abysmal .262 winning percentage.
5. Dick Duff was Leafs interim coach for two games, in 1980.
6. Another trick question: they're all former Toronto players. Joe Crozier (played five games with the Leafs in 1959–1960 and coached 40 games in 1980–1981), Mike Nykoluk (39 games, 1956–1957; 280 games, 1981–1984), Dan Maloney (280, 1978–1982; 186,

1984–1986), Ron Wilson (13 in 1977–1978 and another five in 1979–1980; 310, 2008–2012), and Randy Carlyle (49, 1977–1978).
7. Pat Quinn played 99 games with the Leafs from 1969 to 1970, and coached the team for 654 regular season and playoff games from 1998 to 2006, compiling a .591 winning percentage, the highest in Leafs history.
8. Both Conn Smythe and Punch Imlach hired themselves to coach the Leafs, but only Smythe had the balls — and good sense — to fire himself.

GAME DAY AFFIRMATION

Today I will be my own coach, putting myself in the game whenever I want and praising myself whenever I feel like it. I will also be my own quizmaster and come up with a trivia test that I can actually ace.

GAME 76

Success is the one unpardonable sin against one's fellows.

— Ambrose Bierce, writer and non-Jersey devil

Something terrible happened to Manchester City Football Club in 2012. They won the Premier League Championship.

After a drought that rivalled the Leafs' own Cupless streak (the football club hadn't won a league title in 44 years), Man City actually found themselves on top.

So, what happens when a lovable loser finally finds itself on top of the world? It's a curious question, and one that should give Leafs fans some pause.

For Man City and their fans, success wasn't necessarily that easy to swallow. "I think many older fans feel strangely conflicted by now being one of the teams-to-beat," one commentator opined. "City fans used to be joyful in their misery."

Man City's story is strangely similar to that of our beloved Maple Leafs. The team has a long and distinguished history and enjoyed a Golden Age in the late

1960s, winning a League Championship, FA Cup, League Cup, and European Cup Winners' Cup (all big deals in the soccer world).

The team has also endured numerous lows, including a 1906 scandal where 17 players were banned for accepting more than the league-mandated £4 a week; a long stretch under the leadership of Peter Swales, a Ballardian owner who went through 11 managers in his 20 years; and finally, relegation to football's third tier, which is equivalent to the Leafs being demoted to the ECHL.

And, also like the Leafs, Man City is a money-making machine, with annual revenues in excess of $520 million and a total estimated value of $1 billion — which is almost exactly what the Leafs are worth.

Still, Man City has learned to live with success. Since their Premier League win, the team has been one of the top football (soccer for you neophytes) clubs in England … and their fans have learned to live with success.

GAME DAY AFFIRMATION

Today I will contemplate humility and vow not to let future Maple Leafs successes spoil me. Go ahead, success, try me. I dare you.

GAME 77

I was overlooked long before anyone knew who I was.

— Paul Desmond, legendary jazz
saxophonist and one cool cat

If ever there was a Leafs player who embodies the principles of mindfulness, it was Doug Gilmour.

Just 5 foot 5, Gilmour spent most of his hockey life being overlooked. As a kid, he was cut by a bunch of teams because of his size. At 16, he found himself on his hometown Kingston Voyageurs, a Junior B team, but playing barely three minutes a game. He asked to be released.

By 1981, Gilmour was playing Junior A for the Cornwall Royals of the Quebec Major Junior Hockey League. He had a strong rookie season. But injuries slowed him down, and he was overlooked in that's year's NHL draft.

He went back to Cornwall — now playing in the Ontario Hockey League — and continued to improve, putting up 119 points in 67 games. Still, NHL teams were reluctant to take a chance on the pint-sized phenom. He lasted to the seventh round before the St. Louis Blues picked him up with the 134th overall pick in the 1982 NHL Entry Draft

The following season, Gilmour set the OHL on fire. He led the league in goals (70), assists (107), and points (177) — which remains the third-highest total in OHL history, after Bobby Smith's 192 points and Wayne Gretzky's 182.

Even after that performance, Gilmour had his doubters. The Blues were in no hurry to sign their late-round selection, and Gilmour had already resigned himself to playing in Germany when the Blues finally sent him a contract offer.

It was one the best moves the Blues would ever make. Gilmour scored 25 goals and added 28 assists ... as a defensive-forward. Around the NHL, people realized the Blues had uncovered a diamond in the rough.

Flash forward to 1989 and Gilmour was a now legitimate star with the Calgary Flames organization. But he was still being undervalued. The Flames could not afford to pay him what he was worth, so they shipped him off to the Toronto Maple Leafs in a 10-player deal.

Gilmour quickly became the heart and soul of the Leafs, putting up 127 points in his first full season as a Leaf in 1992–1993 — a franchise record — and adding another 35 points in the playoffs en route to the Conference finals, the team's deepest playoff run since 1967.

Gilmour went on to play five more seasons (plus one game) with the Leafs, finishing his 1,656-game career with 1,602 regular season and playoff points, a Stanley Cup (with Calgary), and two All-Star Team selections. He remains to this day the Leafs all-time leader in assists for a single season (95, in 1992–1993) and total points in a single season (127, that same year). Not bad for a little guy who was thought to be too small to play in the Bigs.

GAME DAY AFFIRMATION

Today I will think of Doug Gilmour as I reframe my mindset, considering all my personal attributes — not in terms of strengths or limitations — but in terms of those elements that combine to make the unique substance that I am.

GAME 78

> *You have to dream before your dreams can come true.*
>
> — APJ Abdul Kalam, former Indian president and potential Winter Warlock understudy

Imagine, The Great One, number 99 himself, gliding across the centre ice with a Maple Leaf on his chest ...

Sound like a pipe dream? In fact, it almost happened — twice.

The first time it wouldn't have been just Wayne Gretzky moving to Toronto — he would have been joined by the entire Edmonton Oilers' roster.

It was back in the 1978–1979, the Oilers' inaugural season, when — according to Oilers' then-owner Peter Pocklington — Harold Ballard approached the team with a bizarre proposition: a full-on, all-team swap, with every Leaf moving to Edmonton, and every Oilers player going to Toronto in return.

Oh yeah, Ballard also wanted $50 million in cash.

Of course, the deal never happened — Pocklington said Ballard just stopped calling.

Fast forward to the summer of 1996. Gretzky — who holds 61 NHL records — had finished his stay with the St. Louis Blues and was a restricted free agent. The Leafs seemed to be the perfect suitor — Gretzky had grown up in nearby Brantford, and he and his dad Walter were both huge Leafs fans.

Apparently Leafs general manager Cliff Fletcher put an offer on the table, somewhere between $2 million and $3 million a year. Even in the face of a separate $8 million-a-season offer from the Vancouver Canucks, Gretzky told Fletcher to get the deal done.

But Leafs management had other ideas.

The ownership group — headed by grocery store magnate and former Ballard crony Steve Stavros — was knee-deep in plans to build a new arena ... and didn't want to put any money toward bringing Gretzky into town.

In the end, the New York Rangers got Gretzky, the Leafs got the Air Canada Centre, Loblaws got Maple Leaf Gardens ... and the Leafs were left with nothing but dreams of what could have been.

GAME DAY AFFIRMATION

Today I allow myself to dream of a past with Wayne Gretzky, a present with $5 beers at the ACC, and a future that unfolds exactly to Shanaplan....

GAME 79

We require, as a team, proper levels of pugnacity, testosterone, truculence, and belligerence.

— Brian Burke, former Leafs general manager and apparent thesaurus owner

And here we are: The Kessel Trade. Or simply just The Trade.

It happened on September 19, 2009. Despite Leafs GM Brian Burke's promise of a patient rebuild, he pulled the trigger on a deal that would send two first-round draft picks and a second to the Boston Bruins in return for Phil Kessel, a promising but untested 21-year-old with a crapload of baggage.

When Brian Burke took over the Leafs as general manager in 2008, there was genuine joy in Leafs Nation. Burke had won a Cup just a year earlier as GM of the Anaheim Ducks and had turned Vancouver turned perennial playoff performers.

But the magic touch had disappeared.

In Burke's six seasons with the Leafs, his teams made the playoffs once (and the less said about that post-season foray,

the better). He had come to town promising truculence —
a $5 word for "toughness" — but instead wound up leaving
a legacy of bad backroom decisions and even worse on-
ice memories.

But it's The Trade that defines Burke's Toronto tenure.

Even though it seemed ill-advised at the time, we Leafs
fans hung in there. It *seemed* like a lot to give up. But draft
picks are a crap shoot at the best of times, so ...

Turns out the first first-rounder was second overall in the
2009 draft: a highly heralded prospect named Tyler Seguin
(who by the end of the 2015–2016 season had already
accumulated 355 points in 426 games, and established himself as a legitimate first-line centre). Meanwhile, with the
ninth pick overall in the 2010 draft, the Bruins took Dougie
Hamilton — a top defensive prospect.

Small consolation that Boston has subsequently traded
both of those players.

Meanwhile, Kessel himself was an enigma. While hardly
a consolation prize, he was streaky, one-dimensional, and
labelled "uncoachable." Yet, he knew how to find the
net: 185 goals in his six seasons with the Leafs, with four
30-or-more-goal seasons (including a healthy 20 goals in the
strike-shortened 2012–2013 campaign).

Kessel was dealt away in the summer of 2015, for a
package that included a draft pick (which they converted to
land goalie Frederik Andersen), a prospect (a good one in

Kasperi Kapanen), and two journeymen (Nick Spaling and Scott Harrington).

And just like that, Kessel was gone, Burke was a distant memory ... and the whole universe (or at least Shanaplan) seemed to be unfolding as it should.

GAME DAY AFFIRMATION

Today I will remember the value of patience. I will think about where I want to be five or ten years from now, and will remember that I need not sell my future for a tiny moment of success in the present.

GAME 80

What a time to be alive.

— Drake, full-time global Raptors ambassador, part-time rapper

2016. A year of change.

Canada welcomed its second Prime Minister Trudeau.

Tragically Hip front man Gord Downie wailed his last on-stage ballad.

And the Toronto Raptors finished with their best record in franchise history. In other words, Toronto's pro sports landscape was shifting. Now, thanks to the Raps, it was not only cool to be a basketball fan, but *rewarding*, too.

As recovering Leafs fans, it may be difficult to suppress our homegrown jealousy. But we must remember that the dinos' franchise history, although shorter, is similarly plagued by tumultuous bad luck that has haunted the Leafs this last quarter century.

The Raptors were conceived in 1995, as part of — along with the Vancouver Grizzlies — the NBA's Canadian expansion. They were, in fact, Toronto's second-ever National Basketball Association franchise: way back in 1946, the newly formed Toronto Huskies played the New York Knicks in the first NBA league game. The Huskies lasted a whopping one season before disappointing crowd turnout forced the team to disband.

In their 21 seasons, the Raptors have only made the playoffs eight times (and gotten past the first round of the playoffs twice). Their all-time winning percentage? A paltry .438, good for 26th best out of 30 active teams.

But 2016 capped a slow rise for the Raptors. Having finished atop the NBA's Eastern Division three times in a row, the team recorded a franchise high 56 victories and .683 winning percentage in 2016.

The future looks bright for the Raptors. So, Leafs fans, let the Raptors' faithful enjoy their moment. It's the right thing, the polite thing, the Canadian thing to do.

Plus, the last thing the Leafs need right now — as they continue with a rebuild of their own — is more bad karma.

GAME DAY AFFIRMATION

Today I will remain gracious and accept that my team shares a city, an arena, and even a fan base with a basketball team. And there is nothing wrong with that.

GAME 81

> *Talent hits targets others can't hit.*
> *Genius hits targets others can't see.*
>
> — Arthur Schopenhauer, philosopher
> and one-man tongue twister

It doesn't always go to plan, or even to Shanaplan. Just ask Tom Martin, Ernie Moser, Randy Osburn, or Steve Bancroft.

Ever heard of them?

Well, every one of them is a former Leafs first-round pick.

Collectively, those young hopefuls played 36 games in the NHL, scoring a total of four points.

And now, as recovering Leafs fans, consider the Holy Trinity of Prospects — Nylander, Marner, and Matthews. We must be mindful that nothing is ever a sure thing.

Consider Alexandre Daigle, a can't-miss superstar in the making, selected first overall by the Ottawa Senators in 1993. After a promising 20-goal, 51-point rookie season, he never topped 26 goals and ended his 616-game career with just 129 goals and 327 points.

At least Daigle had a career. Pavel Brendl was snapped up at fourth overall in 1998 by the New York Rangers, who hoped to cash in on his offensive prowess. Instead, they got themselves a guy who never found his stride in the Bigs. Brendl played just 78 games in the NHL, and managed just 11 goals and 11 assists.

At least Brendl got a look. Hugh Jessiman barely got a cup of coffee. Also drafted by the Rangers — who have made a habit of making crappy first-round selections — Jessiman played just two games in the NHL, for the Florida Panthers, scoring … well, you can guess.

But even Brendl looks like a genius selection compared to Claude Gauthier, Andre Veilleux, and Rick Pagnutti. Drafted, respectively, first overall in 1964 (by the Detroit Red Wings), 1965 (the Rangers), and 1967 (Los Angeles Kings), not one of these can't-miss picks played a single game in the NHL.

So, as we scan the horizon, we must remain mindful.

Sure, the Leafs took William Nylander eighth overall in 2014, and he's already had a strong season in the American Hockey League, scoring 32 goals in 37 games in his first season with the Leafs' farm team, the Marlies … then tallying 13 points in 22 games in a late-season NHL preview the following year.

Sure, Mitch Marner — taken fourth overall in 2015 — captained the London Knights to the OHL Championship and Memorial Cup, racking up 160 points in 77 regular season and playoff games ...

And sure, Auston Matthews was the first pick overall in the 2016 draft, a burly phenom who put together a head-turning season with ZSC Lions of the Swiss National League A — 46 points in 36 games, pretty good for a boy playing against men. He'd come straight from a stellar junior career, scoring 116 points for the U.S. Development Team (he broke — by 14 points — Patrick Kane's single-season record) and earning the MVP and an All-Star Team selection at the 2015 World Ice Hockey Federation U18 Championships.

But that's all in the past. As mindful, recovering Leafs fans we have already learned that the past is irrelevant and the future does not exist. All we have is this moment, and we must live in this moment fully, honestly, and completely.

Still, Auston Matthews looks awfully good.

GAME DAY AFFIRMATION

Today I will be mindful of each moment — each pass, each whistle, each save, each goal — and I will give myself permission to let my heart skip a beat (just a little) every time Auston Matthews touches the puck.

GAME 82

> *There is no real ending. It's just the place where you stop the story.*
>
> — Frank Herbert, sci-fi writer and guy with two first names

All good things must come to an end. Say, October 28, 1993, for example. That's when the longest winning streak in Toronto Maple Leafs history ended. Eleven straight games, starting exactly three weeks earlier.

Or March 10, 1934. That's when the longest home undefeated run in team history ended. Starting on November 28, the Leafs went 18 games — 15 wins, three ties — without a loss.

January 12, 2015: longest losing streak in franchise history — 11 games — ends.

March 1, 2015: longest away losing streak ends after 16 games on the road without a victory.

Or April 22, 1945, when the Leafs' record of 14 straight playoff appearances came to an end with a 2–1 seventh-game Stanley Cup–winning victory over the Detroit Red Wings.

Or February 4, 1968, when Tim Horton missed his first Leafs game in seven seasons, ending his Leafs-record iron man streak at 486 straight games.

Or April 15, 1971, when, after logging 1,298 games in blue and white, George Armstrong's career ended in a 2–1 overtime loss to the New York Rangers.

Or even February 13, 1999. That's when the Leafs played (and lost) their final game in Maple Leaf Gardens.

And this season, too, has come to an end. There were highs, to be sure, and lows. And that distant hum, could you hear it? Did we make it to the All-Star break before the noise became deafening?

That horrible shrieking sound our hearts make when recovering Leafs fans realize that yet another season has come and gone — when, exactly, did you hear it?

In any case, it doesn't matter now. It's Game 82, you've made it through another year, you're a little older and, if not wiser, at least a little more mindful.

GAME DAY AFFIRMATION

Today I will consider my own journey this year, recognizing that while what the Leafs achieved on ice is not a reflection of me as a person. My interpretation of their performance is important to me as person as I grow more mindful of myself and more open to my personal growth.

DRAFT DAY

> *The challenge in Toronto is not to come up with the plan. The challenge is to stick to it.*
>
> — Brendan Shanahan, Maple Leafs president and Lao Tzu in training

We have come full circle.

Another season has come and gone, and we await the Leafs' draft with near-transcendent anticipation.

But if we've learned anything this season, it's that we should not get carried away. We must remain mindful of the process, not focused on the outcome.

Consider the famous fable, the Tortoise and the Hare. It's the story about a wild foot race between two rival animals that the Tortoise ultimately wins due to his perseverance and honesty.

The fable's message has become a mantra of elementary school teachers everywhere: slow and steady wins the race. But the story also contains a deeper, a richer, more mindful message. It's a story about being true to oneself and understanding one's own abilities.

In a way, Brendan Shanahan is our Tortoise and everyone else is the Hare. Shanahan has opted to take things slow, to build a contending team organically through informed draft selections, shrewd player signings, and patience.

This is the Tao of Brendan ... the Way of the Shanaplan.

And there are many important lessons to be gleaned from this Tao:

1. Be honest with yourself (face it: this team sucks).
2. Accept your circumstance (ditto).
3. Recognize your faults, and the faults of your team (where to start?).
4. Take measured action to right what is wrong (what, there's no quick fix?).

Only time will tell if the Shanaplan actually works, but keep the faith: Brendan certainly has history, Lao Tzu, and Aesop's Fables on his side.

DRAFT DAY AFFIRMATION

Today I will take a moment to reflect on the past, with its promises and disappointments, and consider that, no matter what transpired this past season, one truth remains constant: There Is Always Next Year ...

ABOUT THE AUTHORS

Christopher Gudgeon is a screenwriter and bestselling author. He owns seven pairs of Maple Leafs underwear. Follow him on Twitter @1millionmonkies.

Tavish Gudgeon is a producer and screenwriter. He loves the Leafs and refuses to admit he has a problem.

Joey Mauro is a writer, sports junkie, and aspiring mamma's boy. He likes the Leafs but thinks they should draft way more Italian Canadians.

Yusuf Saadi is an award-winning poet, a Raptors lover, and a recovering Leafs fan. He is waiting for the Leafs to sign him to a PTO.

www.ingramcontent.com/pod-product-compliance
Lightning Source LLC
LaVergne TN
LVHW051048080426
835508LV00019B/1769